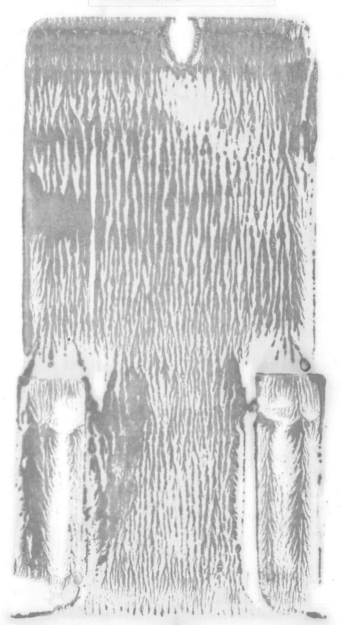

INVENTORY 98

JACQUES BREL IS ALIVE AND WELL AND LIVING IN PARIS

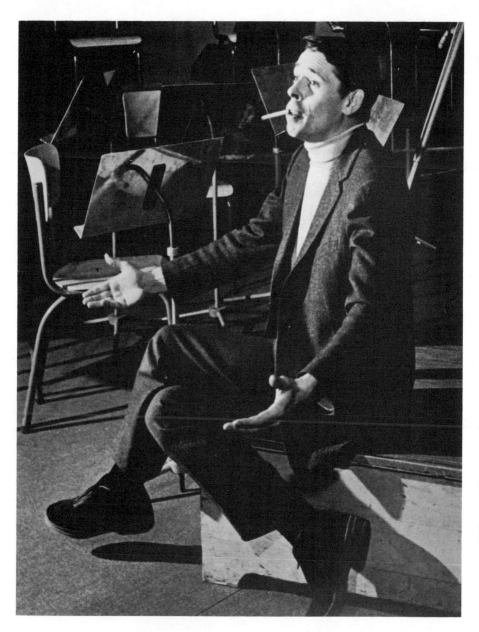

Jacques Brel relaxing during a recording session in 1960.

jacques brel
is alive and well
and living in paris

ERIC BLAU

New York
E. P. DUTTON & CO., INC.
1971

First Edition

Published simultaneously in Canada by
Clarke, Irwin & Company Limited, Toronto and Vancouver

Library of Congress Catalog Card Number: 70-108898

SBN 0-525-13586-3   (Cloth)

For ELLY AND MORT AND JACQUES

And for all those people who came to our show and laughed and cried and made us feel that we were worth something

PREFACE

Jacques Brel Is Alive and Well and Living in Paris has already made a fundamental impression on theatre in general and on the literature of popular song in particular. Its effect on our musical theatre is both interesting and useful. (*Hair* and other stage pieces have used *Jacques Brel* as a model for stage mounting and dramatic negotiation.) *Jacques Brel* as John S. Wilson of *The New York Times* defined it is the first "librettoless musical." The formal concept of the work was simply to use songs as the total text of the play and hopefully, to end with the same sense of fulfillment that a well-made drama should have. That is, to engage, involve, and reveal something to an audience about itself and how it relates to others outside that funny space-time discontinuum we call the theatre.

Yet, historically speaking, *Jacques Brel's* formal innovation is small. Like almost all other formal changes in the arts it extends inherited experience to a greater or lesser degree without losing contact with what has preceded it. It is in the area of its song material that the work is most important. And those songs are the creations of Jacques Brel, written by him over a period of twelve years.

They are important songs—the new art songs of this century.

"They are to American popular songs as *War and Peace* is to *Mr. Roberts*." John S. Wilson, *The New York Times*.

"This is what mid-century popular music should be about, and what the best of it is." Derek Jewell, *London Sunday Times*.

"Brel has captured it all. He is the journalist of the human heart. No, the historian of the human heart." Robert Mayer, *Newsday*.

"Brel's bitter lyricism contains the seeds of revolution." Harvey Perr, *Los Angeles Free Press*.

What does Brel create to make critics and journalists write such praise? He creates art. And in creating this art he burns us with one central idea: human values exceed all others and are superior to all others.

Brel has elevated the popular song to an exquisite height, and he sings to us through his light and darkness without ever blinking or dropping a sentimental tear for some future time when mankind will have inherited the earth.

Mort Shuman and I had the happy opportunity to collaborate with Jacques Brel in order to transform his work into English. What follows is my personal account of how it all happened—including its adventures, problems, and the many people who contributed toward our defiant success.

ERIC BLAU

CONTENTS

JACQUES BREL IS ALIVE AND WELL AND LIVING IN PARIS

I

In November, 1966, Elly Stone was singing at Julius Monk's Plaza 9. That particular night she was proving a point to Mort Shuman, the eminent rock composer and friend of Jacques Brel. Quite simply, she was proving she was the only lady singer in the world who knew what Brel songs were all about and could sing the hell out of them.

Mort was a little uptight about the idea. He was convinced that only men should sing Brel—that Brel's songs were for men only.

In the near dark of the room Mort edgily sucked at his stinking Gitano cigarettes. His great frame made a mountainous silhouette in the middle of the night club. His great curly head was a dark bush in which some pale moonlight had fractured. He was an impressive stranger, and I wondered what he was all about.

Elly sang. Mort applauded. Softly, I thought. "She's good," he said. Then he turned to me, his big face not committing. "The translations are real good."

I thanked him and realized a little belatedly that he was more interested in hearing my lyrics than he was in listening to Elly. I think it must have rankled him a bit that I rather than he had introduced Brel's work into English. If I hadn't, Shuman would certainly have.

(Nat Shapiro, who had introduced me to Shuman and to Brel's work six years earlier, was at the table with us. It was Nat's idea that Mort and I should get together to do some kind of show with Brel's songs. Shapiro was then working for April-Blackwood, a music-publishing subsidiary of CBS. For some time he had been in the international department and had had the occasion to meet Brel. I was not to meet him until March, 1967.)

Mort was also tired of hearing Nat and me telling him repeatedly how Elly was the first performer to sing Brel in English: she had introduced "Ne Me Quittes Pas" and "Carousels" in *O, Oysters!* an Off-Broadway revue I had written and coproduced with Art D'Lugoff. The fact that I was Elly's husband did not help, either. Producer-writer pushes wife—that kind of thing.

Of course Mort never alluded to that point. But I had already become slightly paranoid about it. Elly Stone, one of the truly great singers of the past decade, again and again had to be put down slightly because she was married to slick operator me.

I wanted to tell Mort and Nat and anyone else within earshot that it wasn't a case of Elly trading off me, but the other way around. Elly had been the one—and she is deeply knowledge-able—who, after hearing a Brel recording, had told me that he was not only great but also the most important song writer of the century. She sat with me as I struggled with those early translations. She not only got my syllables in the right places, she also guided the song structure, and taught me about words that sing. In truth, she is the co-author of the first three Brel songs I put into English. And Elly Stone is the one who for the five years following *O, Oysters!* kept the Brel fire burning.

Mort left after the first show at the Plaza. It was November 12th, and he had cut out of the birthday party he was honoring himself with at his apartment on Riverside Drive. He asked us to join him there after Elly did her last show. I generally duck such affairs, but I was curious about Shuman. It was about one in the morning when we got there.

It was the kind of party that grabs the souls of mod movie makers. Or, perhaps, vice versa: the party had been cinematically invented, and the guests had been persuaded that parties should be the way the movie screen had often shown them.

I tried very hard to be invisible with my square suit and bald head, which in that crowded room—a sort of super hippery—was much doomed to failure. Among the maxis and the minis, the beads and open breasts, I was as inconspicuous as a knight in a soft suit of armor. By the way of explaining my presence I kept smiling and saying to those who asked, "I'm a friend of Mort's."

Mort himself reigned with elegance and grace. He moved easily through and among the dancers holding drinks high above the rock-bobbing heads. Although he said "Hiya, Baby!" to every-one who got to his ear or tugged at his pale blue velvet-corduroy coat, it didn't seem he was really with it that night. He was making his party go, but he was not enjoying it. Broad finger-wide strokes of sweat came out of the curly hair and washed slowly down his face. /

I thought that Mort was just as conspicuous as I at this noisy extension of Carnaby Street. For different reasons, of course. I didn't belong at all. He was of it but towering above it; one of the mod princes of a large subculture I did not know.

I watched and thought about him as he danced and played host and Falstaffian bon vivant. We were to be collaborators in Brel—partners. Did we fit?

I was almost twenty years older than Mort. I had gotten involved with French literature when Mort was perhaps seven years old. My own work had been published in France. I had translated the poets Aragon, Eluard, and Masson at their request. But that was back in 1944 and 1945, and my French had become rusty. Mort's French, on the other hand, was superb and he had only taken it up two or three years before. Not only was French beautiful on his tongue, he knew Paris so well he could direct errant French taxi drivers. (Later, when we were in Paris together, I saw him do it.)

Although we were both New Yorkers we were widely separated by our experiences. Mort was one of the creators of the rock generation. More than twenty million records featured his songs as sung by Elvis Presley, Ray Charles, and many others. True, this birthday was his twenty-eighth, and in "gap" terms he was in danger of becoming a dodderer.

My own cultural background was based in the classics and in the left-wing contemporary literature of the 1930s. Unlike Mort, I had never enjoyed success as success is usually measured. As a writer, I felt very much like the twenty-third man on a football squad. Good enough to make the team, good enough to be around and glad to have the chance to suit up, to be on the field of play. It was a living. (Some TV, some film, some books, some publicity, some promotion. The hardnosed grind. Wholesale words, lots of product, enough money to pay the rent, feed the kids, pay the bills and call it a good year when you didn't fall too deeply into debt. The correct American way.)

After hearing Brel and getting to know Brel's work Mort had turned off rock. Brel had wiped him out, and Brel was for Mort a bridge to his own future work. And that's not a small thing because Shuman is an immensely gifted man.

For me, Brel was something else. I knew his importance and

his greatness from the beginning. Although my own attitude toward popular songs had been one of contempt, Brel had proven to me how this old basically ha'penny form could become true art. His work turned me on and sent me on a sentimental journey back to that one year in Paris when I was involved with the chief figures of the French intellectual resistance.

Mort and I had one strong bond in common. We had the innate aesthetic sense to recognize greatness when it slapped us across the face. We loved Brel. Mort loved Brel the creator and Brel the man. I did not know the man; I was quite content to love his work. At that time, at Mort's birthday party, I would not have regretted never meeting Brel. Why spoil a warm feeling?

There were other differences between Mort and me. He is big and outgoing; he dominates rooms; he overrides noise and distraction; he is where it is at.

I am always where I want it to be. In a curious way, although my whole life denies it, I am a romantic. Physically, I'm half Mort. My face is not bland, but mostly it remains cool and distant: Groucho Marx as Buddha. I like to be private until I know where I am at and with whom. I do not commit until I want to commit, and then I drop some of my iron clothing—sometimes all of it. In crowded rooms I stand still until the crowd is aware of me, if they want to be aware of me. In the face of noise and distraction I remain still; and sometimes because I am still, the room becomes still, and my sound, which was there all the time, can be heard.

Feelings override differences. Mort and I were to find that we had far more in common than we would have thought possible when we first met. We had feelings that, in spite of our different life-styles, made us feel good with each other and about each other. Each of us had soul. That is we burned, we seethed. In our private worlds we were wild men: "Fauves" without a Fauvism. The whole world had long since become an awful jungle and who would notice another wild beast or two running? Maybe it was simpler than that. Maybe it was because we were both Jews who enjoyed their Jewishness. (Later that evening Mort and Elly got to the piano and sang Yiddish songs below the level of the rock amplifiers. Perhaps no one else could hear them but me sitting as a silent third on the piano bench. The old songs rolled out sweetly, and Mort was saying and Elly was saying we come from a place and a time that unites us somehow.)

My first really deep feeling of affection for Mort Shuman formed at that party because of a bizarre incident I'm sure Mort has already forgotten.

Good host that he is, Mort had an alcove table heaped high with food. Booze and good French wine were ready to the hand. There was also a large bucket of home-made chopped chicken liver. With some amusement I watched a girl in a floorlength, flower-printed pajama dress scoop up spoonfuls of the chicken liver and pack it down like ice cream into an empty cole-slaw carton. Over her dress the girl wore a ratty fur coat. Covering half her face was a soiled beach hat. Obviously, she was raiding Shuman's larder. I didn't know him very well yet, and I had just geared myself up to the point of small talk. "Hey," I said to Mort, "she's not going to leave enough for the rest of us."

He shrugged.

"Do you know her?"

"I've seen her around," he said. He went to the girl, and there was a lot of passionate whispering. Then Mort walked quickly away from her toward the kitchen. She stopped cramming the half-filled carton and became still while people swirled around her at the serving table.

Mort pushed his way back to her carrying two large Mason jars. He helped the girl fill them with food.

A moment later he had a glass filled with whiskey in his hand, and it was then he walked to the piano where Elly Stone was sitting and began to sing Yiddish songs with her. I think all of that has a lot to do with Jacques Brel.

II

Mort and I began work shortly after his birthday party. It was a good time for both of us. No rips, no tears, no ego involvements. We were doing this for the love of Jacques. If we did not know the final form the work would take, we did know that we were putting into English the most important groups of popular songs in the world at this time. We felt more like surgeons having a ball with transplants than writers.

When we finished a piece, Mort would sometimes call Jacques and sing it to him. Sometimes he would sing to Paris, sometimes to Brussels. I would sit by anxiously not being able to follow Mort's fast French. When the phone was put down, I couldn't help bursting out with: "What did he say?"

Mort, showing little emotion about the opinion of our foreign patient, would shrug: "It's all right. He likes it."

I was never quite convinced. I would pummel Mort with my doubts. "How can he like it? He doesn't understand English very well."

Mort would move his head—half cock, half shrug: "I'll send him the lyrics and a tape."

More protests from me: "What good will that do? He doesn't know English. Someone will have to translate it to him."

"Someone will," Mort said, "but it doesn't really matter."

Shuman must have read the stern perplexity on my face. "Hey," he said, "he trusts me."

"He doesn't know me. He doesn't know a fucking thing about me or about my work. You mean, he trusts you."

Mort smiled; I was amusing him. "That's right," he said, "Jacques trusts me. And I trust you. And what else is there, man?"

I suppose that's no way to run a bank, but it's a good way to live in this world. We never had to discuss the matter again.

The uniqueness of Brel's attitude, his clear browed, non-paranoid way of doing things became apparent again and again in the next few years. Since Jacques is scarcely a certified saint, his insistence on doing "business" this way knocks me out.

Jacques has been wronged, cheated, and screwed often enough never, ever to do business without the aid of fastidious attorneys.

(Mort and I had dinner with Jacques in Paris in October, 1969. Brel had flown in from Switzerland to make the dinner which, while filled with pleasure, was called mainly for business reasons. Charley Marouani, Brel's business manager, was also with us. At last, having reached coffee, the nuts-and-bolts of our business couldn't be delayed.

I took out my carefully prepared sheet of paper and read down the business list point by point. Brel listened carefully. When he did not understand my English—he almost never understands my French!—Mort or Charley would give it a proper translation. Then Jacques would say in solemn camp: Done! So it was Done, Done, Done, Done! sung almost as if out of Kipling. When I had finished my laundry list, Jacques took my hand and set my elbow on the table. "In my country," he said, "when a farmer sells a cow he slaps the hand of the buyer three times." [He did that to my hand.] "Then it is a contract. A sacred oath. Forever." His smile came a split second after a serious meeting of our eyes. I do not know if at that dinner I bought a cow or sold a cow, but the contract—the sacred oath—can never be broken.)

Mort was engaged, as I was, with other projects during those first collaborative months. We knocked off for the Christmas holidays, and we knew we had to suspend work at the beginning of March, for Jacques was coming to do concerts on two successive nights at Carnegie Hall.

Mort had made arrangements to coordinate light cues and other backstage business—a bilingual operation. I purchased some seats. I really cannot sort out my feelings about the prospect of meeting Brel. Partly, I felt that he would not measure up to the greatness of his work. Or, perhaps, he would be overblown and lordly. I guess I wanted him the first way; I'm not sure why.

It's also possible that my deepest concern about meeting Brel was that he would not like me or would simply be indifferent to me. So who was I slipping into his life? I found myself reviewing my own accomplishments as if presenting them to Brel. Sort of off-hand; casual; cool. But the truth is there was nothing much I wanted to say. As the concert approached the uneasiness grew. Whatever Brel's problems might be did not concern me.

The hoped-for-and-feared day came. Mort would cue the lights and Brel would walk out there and open his mouth and sing.

And sing.

And burn.

And leave a scar in the night that would not heal.

We were not there and he was not there. We were arrayed against each other like lights. We were a huge, massive, dark battery cased in red seats throwing our beam against him. He was—what?—a piercing laser. His light through our light. Our light through his light. His brilliance governing, our battery responding—Helplessly, helplessly. All our dignity swelling; all our hopes rising: he was making us human.

The song—issuing. The voice—slightly craggy. The pitch true. The tone ringing with knowledge of places and times, loves, deaths, hurts beyond his words, beyond the language in which not all of the audience could share. Creating a new language we all spoke and understood.

If we were vessels which Brel was filling, he did not fill us slowly. By the third song we were overflowing. Soon we would both cry and laugh, the laughter being only a prelude to more tears. At the end of each song we wanted to release our thunderclap, our mob roar. He would not let us. Our roar would start up but so would the music for the next song and Brel was into it and we choked back our sound and leaned into him.

The first half of the concert came to an end in what seemed to be minutes—or eternities. It was that miracle a great artist can perform: suspend time. Warp time, shape time, until it is tickless, seamless.

Then we *roared*. Except Elly whose hands were limp in her lap, her face ruined by her tears. She did not know if she could survive the second part. She went to the bar for a brandy. She also walked around the block twice and missed the first song after intermission.

In the darkness again; in the light again. The voice spinning out of the body; the body as alive as the voice. His hands comb the air. His legs seem filled with coils and springs. He leaps without moving. He extends; he contracts. He is puking young; he is muling old. He trembles. He sweats. He is shortening his life. I am afraid he will shatter on the stage.

Up in the balcony a woman breaks the tension for us all. She is French. Her voice trumpets out clearly. She hates Jacques Brel. She denounces him as a communist, an atheist, and anarchist, an anti-Christ, an ingrate, and a stinking pig. She asks him to take his odious presence off the stage and out of the United States and go back to Belgium where he belongs.

Brel's hand goes up over his brow as he tries to see her up there. He is smiling broadly. Her barrage continues. The music starts again and she becomes silent. I remember her with gratitude, for we breathed because of her. Now Brel was taking our breath from us again.

Like a flame pumped by a bellows Brel became larger and larger, brighter and brighter, until it all ended quite suddenly. The full stage lights came up, and Jacques was bowing. He bowed, walked off, walked on, bowed. How many times? Many. The tumult; the hero; the ephemeral roar of love. Bow. Bow. Lift an arm—not quite a wave. He smiles the smile of a dead man. No encores; never encores. The program is done.

I watched the theatre empty. The red seats orchestrate themselves into the benign silence that always makes me conscious of my own breathing.

We walked from Carnegie Hall uptown to Harold Levinson's apartment. Levinson, the impresario, had presented Brel and had arranged a small party for friends.

How subdued it was! Not a celebration at all. More like visiting a hospitalized friend. We did not whisper but whatever we said had the quality of whispering.

Jacques sat on the couch between his road manager and his conductor. He slouched between them and looked very small. He sipped at a large whiskey. When someone was introduced to him he pulled himself unsteadily to his feet. Once he tumbled backwards and his whiskey sloshed across his jacket cuff. He was as beat as a forty-year-old fighter whose last strength was used to raise his arms in a victory salute. He said practically nothing to those who congratulated him.

Mort took me to him and said, "This is Eric Blau."

Jacques nodded emptily. Mort asked about dinner the day after next. Brel nodded again. I shook his hand. It was very cold and damp.

I watched him from a safe distance. He resurrected slowly. Time and a few whiskies. In about an hour there was some color in his face, and once or twice he laughed.

III

The dinner date got screwed up. We managed to arrange lunch the day following. It was in a French restaurant on the East Side in the twenties. I had never heard of it but apparently it was well known to gourmets and visiting Frenchmen. Had you cared, you could have learned instantly what acts were being featured at the Bobino in Paris.

When we walked in with Brel there was a lot of *maitre d'* bowing and waiter scurrying. They knew Brel, and his arrival obviously meant something special to the establishment.

Aside from selecting the wine himself, Jacques asked the host to select the food. It was chicken and very good.

He was, I thought, totally restored, for he was very easy to be with and more important, to me, he obviously enjoyed being with us. We sat at the table for almost three hours. For two of those hours we spoke about the show, which at that time had no title and scarcely any shape. Yet none of us seemed to be much concerned.

We sat there amusing ourselves with possibilities.

"How about if we pick songs around which we can write a book?"

"What do you mean *book*?"

"You know, a libretto."

"It's possible, but I don't know if I like the idea at all."

"We have to have some sort of libretto. A form. Otherwise it's concert time, baby."

"What kind of book, do you think? The songs are so good we could get away with any old chestnut."

"What does he say? 'Chestnut'—what does that mean—'chestnut?' "

"An old turkey."

"What?"

"Old fashioned."

"Music hall?"

"No, no. A creaker. Very Oklahoma. Very Hollywood. About this tough young French war vet, see? His heart is broken by this American whore who picks him up in Brussels at the USO. We take the curse off of it by being very realistic. Our whore not only hasn't got a heart of gold, she is a superwhore. She is hustling her way through the whole English army even while the French kid is freaking out over her. And the kid knows it, but he's too hooked to quit."

"I don't know what he's saying. Translate. (Mort here.) Shit."

"We could call the kid Pierre, but everybody would know it's really Jacques."

"Shit. If you want it real, he must get the clap. That makes him suspicious; he mustn't suspect until then. Only at the clap he confronts her. A mandatory scene, that. She explains very logically that it is all quite true. She is a whore, but she loves her work. Doesn't he believe in the equality of women? She is right, of course. He would like to go along, but he is too much in love. Perhaps if she did not screw the English army in entire . . . But the clap is important."

"What did he say, Mort?"

"The clap is important."

"No, the whole thing. (Mort resets it.) But they should part sadly and as friends."

"One more thing. At the end there must be this hard-tender scene where he asks her not to forget him, but if she keeps screwing the English, she must not give up her clap."

"We could give the whole thing an extrapolated treatment."

"Fuck you! I'm not going to translate that."

"You know: production values. Slides, movies, rear projection. We visit the form over the content. We magnify the essence of the songs."

"You may be kidding, but I *was* thinking about projections. Great shots of the sea. Wild. Cruel. Falling out over the audience. Can you see a solitary figure silhouetted against a giant wave?"

"One more time in French, please."

"Love songs against huge nude images. Nothing hidden. Breasts heaving, rumps bobbing, thighs parting. Raw sex, no? A macro-micro closeup of a nipple until it looks like Vesuvius about to explode."

"Stop, you're destroying me. That's a hell of a lot of production value, baby. We'll have to do it on Broadway."

"So? We'll just add a little more production value. Lots of girls. A can-can number with rear-projected crotches."

"Black and white?"

"If in color, add a touch of O'Keefe."

"Or we could do it avant-garde."

"Don't translate. I got that part.

"On stage everybody is really dead. They are all in this great black anteroom of hell. Their lives are played back to them through the songs."

"Hey, great, baby! That's the first time somebody mentioned the goddam songs."

"Pardon me. Songs. Songs. Songs. The onslaught of all this truth slowly but surely breaks them down. Our hero is only a hero *because* all of his life he has wanted to be a fag. But he has never had the courage to give in."

"Aha, a coward!"

"Exactly. Because of the failure of nerve he has lost his chance at mundane happiness. Genuine cowardice has condemned him to eternal damnation."

"What do you think Jean-Paul will say to all of this?"

"It doesn't matter. History will judge."

"You must stick in this other fellow who spent his life begging for alms on the Avenue of the Americas. Actually, he has a Swiss bank account. This is not the reason he is a pig, but slowly we find out that he masturbates, which makes our heroine spit at him."

"Alright, I'll stick him in. But I haven't given much thought to the heroine. But I like very much that she spits at him."

"The heroine is the most degraded. A wife. A mother. Loyal to her husband. He is a physicist who has refused to work for the establishment; so he has worked all of his life for A.S. Beck. . . ."

"Who is A.S. Beck?"

"I'll tell you later."

"He commits suicide when he finds out that he inadvertently sold a pair of sandals to Edward Teller."

"The motivation is not strong enough."

"You've got to see the action: he was kneeling—he was on his knees before Teller. But the real question that remains is: why was his wife loyal? Ask Jacques to answer that one."

"Another bottle of wine, please?"

"What does he say?"

"He says that would not be so easy to figure out. But he likes the idea of having her in hell with the others because it gives the whole gestalt an enigmatic dash."

By and large this meeting drew us closely together as three people working toward one goal. That was very important to me. Theatre projects are always long efforts, filled with dangers, mistakes, misunderstandings, and work tensions that are mitigated only by the quality of the personal relationships of the collaborators. If they don't feel right about each other, the odds for theatrical success, always quite long to begin with, are increased to the point of pain and near-certain failure.

Mort and I were clear on one fact: we knew the importance of Brel's work. Putting the songs into English was an act of artistic importance; putting the songs into English so that they still sang with Brel's voice was an act of artistic integrity. We were determined to achieve that. We knew, too, that even if we could not, in the end, mount a theatre piece, there would be a few dozen new Brel songs to be sung in the United States.

But by whom?

We did not know, and that was why we wanted to do a show in the first place. Not to do a theatre piece, not to present Brel forcefully on a larger scale, would always run the risk of the songs being strangled in the idiot competition of the music industry of the 1960s. We had no intention of turning out hit tunes. Mort had turned out dozens of them, and he wanted none of that. To do the *real* thing was all that concerned us. In short, we were not going to the market; we were going right through the market to establish a new product, one the marketplace didn't offer. (Until rock became the thing the music industry had laughed at it, declaring it worthless. But rock had deep roots in the United States, and while it was music developed by the black community, it was pushing steadily outward into the general musical culture where young people, the principal taste makers of popular music, wanted it, needed it, and dug it.)

Brel's work has its roots in the general ambiance of French music and in the classics. What comes through Brel's sources and talent is something much his own. Taken together with its remarkable lyric sets, Brel songs are new and unique for France as well as the United States. Our guess and judgment was that Brel's work could make it in the United States, provided we could build a place for it. That meant finding a new audience, and theatre presentation was the only way to accomplish it. It was the long way around, and the most expensive way. Looking back, I'm sure it was the only way.

At this lunch Jacques told us he intended to give up concert work. He was bone tired, he said. Empty, empty. He could not give any more.

At that time he was thirty-eight years old. For almost ten years he had been doing some 250 concerts a year. He was also doing a great deal of recording. And writing, too, of course.

He wanted to concentrate on writing and recording. Films, which had always interested him, was another area he wanted to explore both as a writer and actor. (He played in his first later that year.) He had also become interested in the American musical theatre and thought he would like to write a musical one day.

Brel had time to see two musical plays during his one-week stay—*Cabaret* and *Man of La Mancha*.

Cabaret annoyed him, and he left at the intermission. *Cabaret* had been praised as a musical that dealt with a serious theme and brought a level of maturity to American musical theatre. The theme was the rise of Nazism in Germany. It was on this level that Brel was disturbed by the work: it was not nearly serious enough. It was too superficial for the boy who had grown up under the German occupation. For Brel, *Cabaret* had no visceral truth in it; it had not achieved the dimension required by its theme; it was sentimental in the worst sense.

Man of La Mancha, on the other hand, appealed to him greatly for a very special reason. American musical theatre has never been very popular in France. Almost everything attempted there has had a difficult time. Brel related strongly to this musical, for he thought that *Man of La Mancha* could please the French deeply and thus serve to open the French stage to other American musicals. He felt this because Don Quixote is a living literary figure for the European; Quixote is close to the French heart. And the heart is always Brel's prime target.

Brel later acquired the rights to *La Mancha,* translated it, was the prime force in its production, and also played the title role. It was a great success.

But it was not to be a very happy personal experience for him. In making the translation Brel found many ways to improve the play, to give it greater depth, and to do with song lyrics only what Brel can do. This led to many disputes with the American authors and owners of the play. They insisted on Brel conforming very closely to the original text which, of course, is their absolute and unquestioned right.

What it meant to Brel, however, was that he had to settle for work below his standard. In the end, it was Brel's performance as Quixote which made the French *La Mancha* triumph. Disheartened by the experience, sensitive to a loss of personal integrity, Brel closed the show in the early summer of 1969 and decided not to reopen it or play in it any longer. This decision can best be compared to a Broadway producer closing a show after a four-month run, in spite of critical acceptance and long lines at the box office.

I do not remember that either Mort or I protested Brel's announcement that he was ending his concert career. I wonder why, now? Especially after having seen him perform only two days before. Maybe it was because I did not see Jacques' main role as a performer, and I believe that he ranks with the very best in the world. I'm hedging: I think he *is* the best.

Still, performing does not show the Grand Jacques. That is Brel the writer. If he should write no more than the songs already written, he will have left the world a legacy of great beauty that defines man's wasted life and man's hope in this awful century.

I am not sure exactly how long it was after his announcement that I commented on it. "Well," I said, "this is a great opportunity. Now we can separate the performer from the creator. The important thing is that your work must be known."

He was fiddling with a paper match when I said this in my lead-booted French that Mort quickly patched into intelligence. He smiled down at his busy hands. "I'd like that," he said," I'd like it very much."

There is a little irony here. Separating Brel the performer from Brel the creator could be done more easily in English than if his work remained in French. For two reasons. The first is the sheer size of the English-speaking world and its extraordinary communications-media complex. Theoretically at least, it was possible to bring Brel's songs in English to more people than would be possible in all of France and Europe. This possibility exists both absolutely and relatively.

The second reason has to do with the nature of the French culture as it applies to songs. French audiences expect that singers who introduce songs will be the ones to continue to sing them. Thus, only Brel sings Brel. Just as only Brassens sings Brassens; Chevalier, Chevalier; and Aznavour, Aznavour. This usually applies even when the singer does not write the songs he sings but is only the artist who sings them first. It is true enough that some beginning performers and lesser variety talents will sing the songs of major artists. But major artists will not sing the songs of their peers. You will not hear Brel doing Brassens or Brassens doing Becaud or Aznavour. In the United States important performers will not hesitate to sing songs introduced by others.

Mort called an end to the luncheon. He had a date for which he was properly late. We walked west to Park Avenue where Mort left us to hurry downtown a few blocks. I hailed a taxi and rode uptown with Brel to drop him off at his hotel.

I used the opportunity to talk in French. Although I thought I was more fluent since I was less self-conscious now, I was aware of the great concentrated effort Jacques was making to understand me.

I was saying that these buildings that we passed did not exist only a few years ago. That the city kept tearing itself down and thrusting up new. And that I found it unnerving. I hated to see old landmarks go. I asked him if he understood, and he said "Yes."

What really got to me, I said, was the loss of the places of childhood. The entire district, the immediate neighborhoods, whole streets, houses, names, and all had vanished since the 1920s.

He cut in and asked in French, "The house in which you lived as a boy, it doesn't exist? You can't go there to look, to walk about?"

I shook my head.

His reaction was all in the way his head lowered and his mouth twisted. "That's very sad," he said, "I can go back. The house in which I was born still stands. One must go back once in a while. It is very important, that."

We got to his hotel, and he hopped out. We shook hands through the open door. It would be more than two years before we would meet again.

IV

I think it is remarkable that Jacques Brel exists at all. By all logic, right, and chance, he should never have emerged.

I know a few things about him, for I have read, I believe, most of the intelligent things written on Brel. But it is not enough. Sometimes, involved with his work, it seems suddenly that I know him completely: everything he is; all of his life and all of his secrets. After all, all of it is in his songs. But that is the trouble with art. It lets you know everything at once, and then it withdraws into mystery and makes you come back to it.

So let me tell you what I can about Jacques Brel. He was born in Brussels on February 8, 1929. In trying to account for what he later became, various journalists and biographers refer to his childhood as being especially ordinary. He was born into a middle-class Catholic family. His father was a manufacturer of cardboard and cartons. The name Brel had long been familiar to people in Brussels and other parts of Belgium because it was painted on truck panels and printed on the products of his father's factory. Apparently there was no special emphasis on music or literature in the Brel household.

Brel's childhood is best described in his song "Mon Enfance," underscoring the fact that his formative years were anything but ordinary. His background in a family sense was ordinary, perhaps, but not his childhood. (But that reference to family background only makes sense in narrow sociological terms. To the child it was all unique. Is not the family unique to every child?)

I think of him as a small child with enormous eyes. Not the eyes of a still camera, but of a motion-picture camera dollying forward from the big overstuffed chair where he sits. He is trying to see his family, trying to understand and relate to them. Unable to do this, he feels isolated and frightened. Yet he has the cinema of memory which he will later play back and understand with devastating insight.

But at the earliest age Brel seems painfully aware of his isolation from the very group, his family, with which he wants to be most deeply joined. The family should give him security and love; he wants this desperately. But all they seem to offer is a physical environment with mundane comforts; a place for him in which feeling is lost. Their concerns always seem to be about business, about class and social status, about the future and how it is measured out in success, estates, and inheritances. He intuits, almost as a tribal being, that he is included in their concerns and plans, not as a living being, but as an object. He knows viscerally that they take it for granted he will grow up to become one of them. He already sees his family as a group of pre-ghosts plodding toward extinction and offering him all "the solutions which will be without love."

No, not an ordinary child, but a very special one who retreats into silence and shyness to plan his survival—if he can somehow find an escape route to life.

He was given the very best education afforded to children of the affluent upper middle class. But his schooling was accomplished largely during the war years, while Belgium was under Nazi rule and Brussels was gray with oppression. His adolescence passed in a land where there was no joy, where laughter was careful, and Brussels itself seemed to be an ancient ruin, a dead city, its citizens like passengers in a great station waiting the arrival of a train.

The six war years passed, and the boy's private terror began to crystallize. Everything was automatic. He joined his father's business. The next years would be used to prepare him as heir apparent to the cardboard-carton enterprise. Since there is nothing else he wants to do at that time, the boy submits to his destiny. (Later, he told me that the clearest memory he has of the thousands of things that go on in a small plant is of his stenciling cartons and remembering that he enjoyed it.)

Two important things happen for Brel at this time. First, there is the awareness that music and literature, which always attracted him deeply, were emerging in a new way for him. He did not want merely to enjoy them; he wanted to involve himself, he wanted to create. Secondly, life in the factory troubled him. Day by day, year by year, men and women invested their lives into a routine without meaning. How was it possible for people to live this way, he wanted to know. He felt a prisoner and he wanted out.

Go where? Do what? Jacques Brel, at the age of sixteen, had made one visit to Paris. Even in Brussels, or perhaps especially in Brussels, Paris was a legend and the true center of all things. But Brel found the post-war city cold and uninteresting and he disliked it. He went home to his work in the plant.

Yet, even as he returned to Brussels he knew that he must exist outside the cardboard life that had been planned for him.

He began to write songs. (I wonder about this: why songs? Why not novels? Why not poetry? Plays? Films? For he is mainly a writer of words. My guess is that he opted for the song because it seemed direct and easy and safer to attempt. What a glorious error he had made! He would soon learn that songwriting on his high level would be murderously difficult. Poets, of no less stature than Louis Aragon, had tried their hands at it with indifferent success.) Thus he began his voyage away from a life he was sure would destroy him. To his family and friends it seemed he was giving up everything to write songs—clearly a tragic waste!

He sang these first songs more or less informally before youth groups and charitable organizations in Brussels. Brel also cut his first disk. Neither the live performances nor the recording worked out very well.

There is no sign (although it must be so) that his first attempts to sing his songs were unsatisfactory. Did he rationalize those first experiences? Did he find himself "marvelous"? Probably not; at the height of his success, he is a cool self-critic and filled with doubt that he has ever said precisely what he has wanted to say. He is plagued by the constant fear that next week he will be unable to say anything at all.

His decision at the end of that tentative time is quite clear, however. At the age of twenty-three Brel severed his association with the family business. He went to Paris. Everything was there; it was the big wheel. It was filled with composers, writers, entertainers, places in which to entertain. You could learn there; you could test yourself there; you could flower and grow there. Or you could die there.

That's what almost happened.

He came to Paris with his wife, Michelle, whom he had married when he was twenty. They had two infant daughters. He had married without his family's approval. By their lights he should have married within his class instead of marrying someone who could not improve his position.

Jacques and Michelle settled in a working-class suburb outside of Paris. They had very little money and Brel neither wanted, nor could he expect, any help from his family in Brussels. His suburban home was a decrepit, jerry-built wooden shack. It had nothing to recommend it except its very low rent. It had no running water. They had the use of a communal pump in the back courtyard.

The first weeks were exhilarating. He was free, and he knew that he wanted to write. He did not feel the need to perform. He wanted his songs to be sung.

Brel learned quickly enough that his work was not of great interest to the publishers or singers of Paris. He dutifully made the rounds, but it was becoming clearer that he would have to sing his songs himself if he wanted them heard. His guitar playing was not bad, but clearly not professional. He sang in a strong baritone, but it lacked grace and control; and as an actor in song he was hardly more than an amateur. Brel knew that he had to put all those elements together to become a performer.

He could use Brassens as a model. It should not be too difficult to perform as well as that big, burly, mustached *chansonier,* who walked out on the stage and sang his own songs in a quiet, straightforward way. Brassens sang almost as if there was no audience there, never trying for effects or bigness, just letting the song go with his soft voice and nicely controlled guitar. Yet the audiences hung on every word.

But Brassens would not be useful to him as a model. Brel's instincts were completely different. In working with his guitar and with his voice, in finding himself as a performer, Brel was shaping something new, something only he could be.

The work was very hard, and life in the hovel did not make it easier. There were unimagined privations for Brel and his family. For the first time in his life Jacques began to know illness; his teeth began to go bad. He didn't mind the necessary extractions as much as the frequent pain.

It was a feverish race against time, health, and hope. Jacques worked at his act and simultaneously made the rounds. He auditioned for publishers and night-club owners. He struck out with the publishers, and somewhere past his hundredth audition he got himself a job at *Les Trois Baudets* (The Three Asses) where Brassens had once sung.

And what did that mean? Everything at that moment. He was on stage. He could get up and sing his songs. The trip from Brussels to the dark of Les Trois Baudets had taken more than three years.

In a show-business sense it was no triumph. What he had been told in those empty years of auditioning was that he was a nice kid, but that he was not really with the Paris scene. He was a Belgian rube, a hayseed with a Brussels accent. At Les Trois Baudets, in spite of all his work and effort, he still seemed to Parisians to be a kid from the country. The songs he sang were open and simple ones showing his pounding heart pinned openly to his black turtlenecked sweater. Yet Brel was all real and Parisians sniff out realities as expertly as hogs root out truffles. They liked the skinny kid. He gave them something, and they gave him something. For Brel it was not only a chance to work but a chance to know them, these Parisians, below their cool, sophisticated exteriors.

The Parisians, who seemed so complicated and so distant from the passionate young Brel, were not as cold as they seemed. He learned they were armored to protect everything soft and tender inside them. They were not really so different from the Flemings and Walloons of his own country.

He learned one thing more from the Parisians: they would not and could not accept the heart alone. The heart had to be mixed with the head; passion had to be allied with reason. His songs began more and more to reflect this mixture. If the mixture turned out to be explosive, it was because Jacques kept truth and compassion in his work.

The changes in the nature of his songs—they were both hotter and cooler, lighter and darker, but always subtle and complex even when they were almost pure bursts of passion—"Marieke"—were coincident with the growth and change in Brel.

A year after Les Trois Baudets Jacques made it to the stage of the Bobino, the old music hall where so many French immortals started and still perform. He was scrounging out a living now. The critics began to take note of him. They were gentler now about his being a small town boy in the big town. They approved of his natural, unpretentious performance, and his songs, they observed, were good.

It was in 1957 that Brel made the Bobino and from that point on his career flowered.

I know that whenever he sits in the dentist's chair he must savor the irony of it all. He had come to Paris to write. In order to write he had to learn to perform. In performing he became one of the greatest entertainers who has ever walked on a stage. Then he gave that up to concentrate on writing because at the age of thirty-eight he no longer had the driving energy to do both.

However, his mounting success did not follow the ordinary show-business route. Again Brel did something quite extraordinary. He didn't enjoy the idea of being the darling of Parisian sophisticates. The idea of playing the Lido and Olympia and accommodating to the big time had its dangers. Brel knew he was developing the song in a new and better way, and he believed greatly in the value of the popular song. He wanted his work to belong to the people. ("I never sing for audiences; I sing for people.")

That is an interesting desire because in these times songs (and many similar art "products") belong to the copyright owners, i.e., music publishers. They are interested in how much money a song can earn. This may, offhand, seem to show that the creator's desire and the publisher's desire are exactly the same: bring the songs to the people, and then the people will have the songs, and the publishers and writers will have the money. Everything even Steven. But there is a qualification: publishers want it all to happen quickly and easily. (The hit song thing.)

But Brel did not believe that things happen easily. Why should he? To him only the hard way seemed real. Perhaps it was the only logical way. His entire life had impressed him with that.

His belief in his songs coincided with his belief in himself and his need to know that others could believe in him and his songs. So he decided to bring them those songs and his life. He spent almost ten years at it.

Brel went on the road. He stayed on the road all but two months of each of those ten years. He sang in hairy bars and converted movie houses, in barns, and beer halls, and churches. It was a process of criss-crossing the entirety of France. He wore out two cars a year in this process. The rube was singing for the rubes, bringing them some of the most sophisticated and ballsy material ever written. And Brel knew what Paris did not know. He knew that no matter how complex his song structures might be, all of them were gut simple in their feelings. He knew that any longshoreman or any farmhand could feel his laughter or his tears because they were all locked in the same miserable little world. And whom was he singing about in "Amsterdam," "Jef," "La Statue," "Madeleine," "Mathilde," etc., if not them and himself?

The two-hundred-odd concerts he performed each year were sung in the most outlandish places. At first, of course, it was only Jacques Brel coming to lands-end to sing. And who was what's-his-name anyway? And was he worth two or three francs to hear? (Brel wanted the contact with that skeptical audience most of all.)

Later, as his fame grew, he continued his touring and always returned to the places he had been. He now appeared before the same people as a national hero. For most of his audiences Brel was the only major live entertainer they had ever seen and heard in their home towns. (Brel's later appearances had the same impact, let us say, as would Frank Sinatra's if Sinatra were to play annual or biannual concerts in Shushan, New York, or in Cheyenne, Wyoming.)

And yet, with the growth of his fame and the growth of the fees he could demand, Brel played for the hinterlands only at prices they could reasonably afford. In simple bookkeeping that meant if Brel played the Lido for one month, he could earn more than he could on the road in a year.

Was Brel, then, some kind of altruistic, pioneering bleeding-heart nut? Far from it. It was from these people and in these towns that he learned much about the way to make songs. He learned more about the validity of a song in the unsophisticated backwoods of France than he could possibly learn in the ultra-sophisticated backwoods of Paris whose judgment he never quite learned to trust anyway.

During this arduous touring Brel was finding a new approach to the popular song. He was transforming it into an art form— not just for France but also for the rest of the world. He was hooking up with a tradition that had all but disappeared from popular culture. In contemporary terms he was doing no less than the *lieder* composers of a century before. He was bringing the "art song" back into the mainstream of French cultural life. Mencken to one side, he had proved that you could succeed without underestimating the taste and intelligence of the people.

He was accomplishing this not only through his art but also through the great determination and physical energy he brought to his work.

Why?

His work had become his life.

And Jacques Brel is a man in pursuit of his life. He hunts for it with every bit of his art. Sometimes he encircles life, but it escapes and he must hunt again. He is a running man who does not run away from life; he runs toward it. He is unarmed and vulnerable and afraid, deeply afraid. But not of wounds or of dying, but of not finding, of not realizing at last who he is, who we are.

It is a lonely art, a lonely search—yet a search in which his tenderness will not be destroyed.

V

And Brel will deny every bit of it.

When he is asked if he thinks The Song is a major or minor art form, he says, in his opinion, it is neither; it isn't an art form at all. It is a craft, and he is a craftsman.

To emphasize this point he mimes a carpenter at work with a saw and plane.

Then he will discuss the hard technical demands made by the process of song writing. You fashion a lovely line carrying a good thought. As a line it sits very well and you might be satisfied with it. But you find it does not quite serve the tune and the tempo, and you must carpenter it. Although you do not want it to happen you have changed your lovely line and perhaps impaired the thought.

Also there is the problem of the way the words and music fit the voice. If neither rests within the capabilities of a good musicianly singer, it will not be a song worth singing; one, perhaps, that cannot be sung. So more carpentry is needed.

Finally, there is the matter of the contemporary song itself, one written to be sung to people now who want to hear and experience it in terms of their own lives. How does it lend itself to performance? Does it communicate; does it work? If it doesn't, you have failed and must throw it out. If it works in part and holds promise of success, then back to the shop for more carpentry!

But all of that is probable nonsense. Brel hides behind his walls of craft because he is very uncomfortable at being called either an artist or a poet. How *much* an artist he is can perhaps be seen in the following account.

He was complaining about the attitudes of the authors of *Man of La Mancha* when he was translating it. At one point Quixote says in English: "I am a poet." Brel translates this into French as *"Je suis presque un poète."* (I am almost a poet.) He does this for good reasons. One is that being a poet in the French literary and popular mind is the supreme accomplishment. (Picasso once told me he would much rather have been a poet than a painter.) It is for others to say: "He is a poet." The poet himself will sidestep and say, "I am almost a poet, I try to be a poet, or I write poetry," but not baldly, "I am a poet." It would be like a performer saying, "I am a superstar."

Another reason for Brel's translation was that it fitted Quixote's character much better. But Brel could not convince the authors of this. They wanted it as it had been written. So if it would be immodest for Quixote to say, "I am a poet," how can Jacques Brel admit he is an artist?

Another question: are song texts poems? Brel's answer is no, and I agree very strongly.

Pop critics are endlessly designating some lyric writers as poets. There is not a single lyric writer in the United States, Canada, or England, of whom I know, who can be regarded a poet. One has only to read their texts stripped of the music to realize the truth of this. Even where we find an honest-to-goodness-poet writing a song lyric, it does not follow that the lyric is a poem.

What are the differences between song lyrics and poems? I will cite some.

Song texts are partial works needing both music and performance to transform them into a significant whole. Poems are structured solely of words and are complete in themselves.

Song texts are limited tools with which to explore human experience, values, and emotions. Poems are far more versatile as sensors and are practically unbound by subject, complexity, depth, inventiveness, and even length. It would take several months to sing *Paradise Lost* if a song form could be devised for it, and, of course, no singer could do it. A song lyric is a wind-up clock. A poem is a wind and a water that tells time.

Song texts must use words open enough to use music tolerable to the singing mouth, throat, and tongue, arranged to avoid consonant and vowel collisions and awkwardnesses for singers, and which come to the ear of listeners with great intelligibility. Poems use words that are often freighted with a dense music of their own. Poems use words often with a light regard for the reader's ability to vocalize them, counting on the sound of the poem words to go through the eye into the head to take sensual shape there. Poems use words in thicker, more complicated patterns embracing image, idea, and sensuousness all at once, and require a reader who is in some way already prepared to embrace the work. (Because of this demand on the reader there are fewer readers of poetry than other written forms, and certainly far fewer readers of poetry than listeners to songs.)

Song texts, when they are employed, are locked into rhythmics and tempi, which by the very nature of the song must repeat. Poems are not locked by rhythms and tempi but may move freely from pulse set to pulse set as the particular work requires.

But the main difference between song lyrics and poems is found in their individual planes of existence. It seems to me that a poem may brush heaven while a lyric has a mundane limp.

But a song may also brush heaven and probably does so far more often than a poem. This, however, requires the marriage of words, music, and performance. So while a song text, a lyric, should not be mistaken for poetry, the song as a whole can achieve greatness and become art.

In this sense Jacques Brel is a great artist. And in this sense his denials do not matter one bit. That evaluation is for others to make.

In all other matters Jacques speaks for himself.

Life has taught him he must be ready to do everything with his own hands and alone. At the same time, he actually enjoys working with others, and some of his most successful songs have been collaborations. Jouannest, Corti, and Rauber have co-composed or have totally composed music for his words. The song texts are always by Brel.

His generosity, in a professional sense, is unusual. Mort and I had finished the translation of "My Death." It was a close trans-fer from the French to the English. But we thought that the music missed something. Mort, knowing Brel far better than I, said, "I'll change the tune. He won't mind." So Mort did and sent a tape to Jacques. Jacques' answer came: "You've improved it. It's better than mine."

I was totally stunned by the response. Had it been me, I would have been quite annoyed. It takes a secure man, a free man, to act so openly, so generously.

When you pass from private into public life, everyone wants to know what you think about everything. Since Brel has no publicists inventing and reinventing his image, he has had to express his views endlessly.

"What are your politics?"

"Far left."

"Are you a communist?"

"No."

"Your religion?"

"I am an atheist."

"What are your pleasures?"

"Smoking cigarettes, drinking whisky, listening to classical music, and flying my plane."

But what he feels and believes is to be found in his songs. Not the total Brel, but as much of himself as he can offer—the essential Brel. So true is this of Brel's songs he must very often deny that each of the characters he creates in his songs is actually himself. He is not the drunk in "L'Ivrogne," or the matador in "Les Toros," neither the schnook nor the fag in "Les Bonbons," etc. Yet his song characters are so beautifully drawn and so invested with dramatic truth, it is almost logical they should be mistaken for him.

Not infrequently, someone will say that Brel writes protest songs. This drives him up walls. He doesn't write protest songs, but those who protest may find anthems in the Brel works. And it is also true that Brel cannot help writing songs that protest loudly. But this is the awful cry of a man in pain, not the small beep of a tune directed against an immediate set of inequities. The protest song, in a partisan way, pricks. A Brel song, in a nonpartisan way, explodes. Brel offers everyone only one choice: to reclaim his own humanity.

But how does one reclaim his humanity? That's complicated, isn't it? Brel has only his songs to offer toward this hope, and songs are never enough. A song cannot stop a war, nor can it slow the processes of our dying. Yet, one hopes that some songs can change some men, and some men can change others, and who knows what good might result?

When Brel wrote "Les Flamandes" it rocked Belgium totally. It was neither a political nor a protest song. Somehow it questioned the whole fabric and quality of Belgian life. (*Why do Flemish girls dance on all the ringing Sundays? Because their parents told them, their teachers told them, the priests and the bishops told them that they must repeat the lives handed down to them. Get engaged, get married, have children, wait for the old folks to die, inherit their estates, and repeat and repeat and repeat forever the inane ritualistic emptiness of their prefabricated lives.*) It was true and cutting, and Brel felt the wrath of his countrymen on all levels. He did not play in Belgium for a year after the release of "Les Flamandes." Nor did they forgive him until he wrote "Le Plat Pays" (The Flat Lands).

"Le Plat Pays" is not only a great song, but it is also the true anthem of Belgium. A new kind of anthem, beautiful, graceful, stately, and devoid of the cheap patriotism of anthems as we know them. Belgium as it was, as every Fleming and Walloon knows it truly to be. (*Where the cathedrals are our mountains of stone, where their dirty black steeples touch heaven alone, where*

stone gargoyles hook the passing clouds, where the days of our
years flap like shrouds, and the roads of the rain how they can
burn, on the West wind, west wind hear it yearn; this flat land
that is mine.)

Brel must be the only maker of songs in the history of the world who destroyed a nation with one song and resurrected it with another.

The Belgians did not forgive him for "Les Flamandes," and he did not forgive them for not forgiving him, nor did he want them to forgive. He wanted his people to accept "Les Flamandes" because it was true.

But it wasn't easy. The government pressured him not to sing it in his Belgian concerts, although he had already recorded it and it could be bought. For a while he did not sing it, but the censorship rankled. If he could not sing "Les Flamandes" in Belgium where it had its true meaning, what good was the damned song? Nobody got uptight about "Les Flamandes' when he sang it in Paris.

So he made up his mind to sing it at the University of Leuven (Louvain), one of the oldest and largest Catholic universities in the world. He was specifically cautioned not to sing "Les Flamandes" but he gave no reply to the warnings. Special details of police were on hand in the auditorium—to protect whom? They were arrayed along the aisles so that Brel could see them from the stage. They had clubs they tapped heavily into their gloved palms.

Of course, Brel sang the song. What else could he do? He closed the first half of the concert with it. There was dead silence in the hall—no applause, no boos, no cheers. The students let Brel confront the police alone.

When the concert resumed the audience responded to him as they always do: applause, roars, shouts, cheers. But on that night it was not enough. So to close the concert he sang "Les Flamandes" again.

This time the students did not hold back. They joined him and set up a great, great cry to the close Flemish heavens. The police melted away. Now "Les Flamandes" was no longer a battle cry. It was just another song Jacques had created. Something beautiful, something true. And it no longer mattered if Brel sang "Les Flamandes" in Belgium.

Time after time I think about the songs he writes and wonder what his secret is. I also know that I will not discover it any more than Jacques will. It is because he somehow creates art, and art by its nature includes the mystery and wonder of its own birth.

Of course, you can ask Jacques how he works at his songs, and he will tell you that he sweats them out. He has some fifteen or twenty songs in process on his stand-up work desk at all times. He works them over repeatedly as he questions each word and its placement. Given a year he will have completed eight or ten songs. His working process is of interest only because of the results, but I really cannot be sure that there is a meaningful relationship between them.

So Mort and I were holding this marvelous bag of Brel works. We were its guardians. But that first enthusiasm of doing the translations had passed, and now we had to do a show.

I had no real vision, no grasp, no idea of what would transform thirty songs into a threatre piece. Frankly, I was bugged, puzzled, and fearful of the whole situation.

VI

The months after Brel's departure from us were filled with events that had a bearing on the show, or on which the show had a bearing. In that limited sense they were important, but they seemed to sequence themselves in slow motion. There was progress —but no progress. The show had no form. This bothered the hell out of me. I cannot understand a work that has no form.

It has always seemed to me that content in a play, or in any of the arts, does not really exist without form. Without form, content is defrocked and holds no office. Form without content reduces itself to style. At the extreme, I think, content without form becomes overly tendentious statement making, while form without content becomes merely a product for industry. (Cinema, publishing, theatre, music; it doesn't matter. The industrialized lively arts need a product, and a product, in this sense, is something that can be easily duplicated and rushed to the market. That's where the money is, and that's what the business is all about.)

The product makers in the arts do not eschew content. They simply cannot wait around for it and remain in business. Thus the mandatory emphasis on style and technique—the packaging. It seems to me that there is bitter irony here because in the end these packagers of art are left with no real understanding of form. That is why on many notable occasions the whole market slips away from them, and they take a well-deserved bath.

Quite the opposite is true when content is used without form. In an art sense content only becomes content when it reveals ideas and emotions of which we are not aware except as we are made aware in and through the presented art context. Form serves to reveal and unlock content, while content, revealed and unlocked, devours form. There are no demarcations between form and content in any work that has achieved art; art is seamless.

We had no form, not a notion. But we did have a title. Nat Shapiro invented it. Later, he disliked it so thoroughly he proposed several others not nearly as good. None of us cared for his first idea either, but in the end we were stuck with it. (When the show succeeded, I suspect we all began to believe the title was brilliant.) All the same, it was very comforting to have some title—any title. It almost made us believe we had a show.

Others believed it too. It was enough for Mort and Elly to sing the songs to get us producers.

We had the choice of several, but in the end it was 3W Productions, my own firm, which presented *Jacques Brel Is Alive and Well and Living in Paris*. However, I had not wanted 3W to produce it.

3W Productions was spanking new at that time, and I did

not relish a situation where my firm would be presenting a work of which I was co-author and in which my wife was going to be costar. It all smacked of collusion and conflict of interest.

Besides, we wanted 3W to produce *Hair* and Ionesco's *Amédée* as its initial ventures. (Henry Hoffman, one of the four associates in 3W, was to say later on, "My God, think what it might have meant if we had produced *Hair, Amédée,* and *Brel* in one season; we would have become the most important producers in the country over night!")

It was a fair observation so an explanation of why we did not produce *Hair* and of the sad fate of *Amédée* is in order.

I had gotten to know Gerry Ragni and Jim Rado through my former wife, Isabelle, who worked with them in the Open Theatre. They had become close friends and would sometimes drop by our apartment on 92nd Street on Sunday afternoons. We would have something to eat, and somehow it always seemed to be cream cheese, bagels and lox, smoked white fish, herring, Danish and coffee. When we first met, three or four years before they had written *Hair,* Jim and Gerry were close cropped, wore square suits, and did not remotely imagine that one day they would set theatre on its ear.

They were actors—very good actors—and were also very serious about theatre. Jim had already played quite successfully on Broadway, and while Gerry had not performed uptown, he was well known Off-Broadway and highly regarded. Unlike most actors, they were far more interested in the nature of the theatre than in their personal careers as actors. They were also very much aware of the world in which we lived, and most of our talk would shuttle between social problems, politics, and threatre. I would never lose the opportunity to read them new Brel translations, and I would have been disappointed if they had not approved.

It was through Isabelle that I had learned Jim and Gerry had written the book and lyrics for a musical work, and it was through Isabelle that the authors of *Hair* asked if I would read the first draft.

It turned out to be a very interesting, sometimes brilliant, sometimes powerful script having a number of faults, as almost all adventurous creations do. The book was cumbersome; the lyrics ranged from very good to extraordinary; and they had no music for it. Even at that time it was clear Jim and Gerry were on to something. We talked in great detail about the book, and I tried to suggest ways to make it stand.

We all agreed that what they needed most was a composer. Getting the lyrics set, and hearing the music would certainly offer approaches to fixing the book. Jim and Gerry had tried writing their own music, and it hadn't worked. Jim had once performed with a rock group and had a musical background, but wasn't really a composer.

I suggested they get together with Galt McDermott, a Canadian composer, living in New York, who was deep in a rock-and-country bag and very gifted, I thought. Galt and I had sporadically tried collaborating on songs but with no success. My texts and Galt's music just didn't want to get together. It seemed to me that he would be eminently right for Jim and Gerry's *Hair*.

I also suggested that Jim and Gerry meet with Nat Shapiro, since it was Nat who had introduced me to Galt. The idea was not only to have Nat get them together with Galt, but also to think positively about having Nat manage them as a team. Nat was one of the best people I knew in the music arena and the very successful manager of Michele LeGrand. So within the next week I had arranged for lunch with Jim, Gerry, Nat, and myself at Downey's. I reviewed the situation for Nat, suggesting that he get in touch with Galt. That's how that part of the *Hair* operation got started.

In the meantime I had told my associates about *Hair*-in-progress. So one hot night in July, Henry Hoffman and I went down to one of those mid-Manhattan rehearsal halls to hear the first audition for *Hair*. Twenty or thirty people were there when Galt, mopping his brow at the piano, started up the music. Jim and Gerry, with a little help from some young actresses, went through the songs, some of the scenes, and a narration of the libretto. It still lacked clarity, but it was now fantastically exciting. Galt, Gerry, and Jim had jelled explosively. Henry Hoffman was humming "The Age of Aquarius" as we walked up Eighth Avenue later. I think he was the first member of a *Hair* audience who went out with one of the hit tunes in his head.

I asked him, "What do you say, Hank?"

"Let's produce it," he said, "It's got a lot."

I told Jim and Gerry that we were ready to do it, and they could have contracts immediately. But a very large fly had already entered the ointment. Joe Papp had been at the same hearing. He wanted to present it as the first offering of the New Public Theatre on Lafayette Street. What's more, Papp would guarantee an eight-week run.

In face of this development, Jim, Gerry, Isabelle, and I had another meeting on 92nd Street. 3W or Papp? It seemed plain to me that Papp's offer was the one that they had to take. To have the sponsorship of a new and important nonprofit theatre organization, and to be its initial attraction was not to be resisted. I told Jim and Gerry if I were them I would have to go with Papp. I pointed out that if 3W did the producing, all we could guarantee would be to open the show. But if it didn't score, we would have to close it damned quick. Papp was giving them eight weeks for sure.

Hair opened in the Public Theatre to mixed notices. The reviewers loved the score and songs but faulted the book. Yet they knew that something big had happened. A fresh, vigorous wind had literally blown the old concepts of musicals out of the theatre.

Jim, Gerry, and Galt knew the faults of the work, and they set themselves to revising it. After the Public Theatre run Michael Butler took over as producer. He moved the work to the Cheetah, a rock and go-go place where, strangely enough, *Hair* didn't fit. It had problems there too. The form, like the form for Brel, had not yet presented itself. This did not happen until after we had opened *Brel*, and not until Tom O'Horgan came on the scene to redirect and restage it for Broadway. The history of *Hair* is very well known from that point on.

Henry's observation about how important 3W would have been if we had produced *Hair* was, I think, a bit romantic. It took a Michael Butler to turn the trick, and we didn't have that kind of money even if we did have some courage and belief. In theatre, guts alone is never enough.

Meanwhile, back at 3W, we were working on the pre-production problems for *Amédée*. We were interviewing directors, and because of the very spectacular stage effects required, we were paying equal attention to designers. At the very center of *Amédée*'s action there is a pair of giant legs, belonging to a corpse, that grows fantastically and smashes through walls. I was convinced we needed a designer who also was an engineer.

Stanley Swerdlow, a 3W associate and a friend of Eugène Ionesco, had acquired the rights to *Amédée* a year before our production company was formed. Stanley was devoted to getting *Amédée* staged.

Amédée is, perhaps, Ionesco's most important play. It had never been staged in the United States except in workshop form in the mid-fifties. Swerdlow, tall, big boned, heavy set, and who at first brush seems as square as Miami Beach in winter, is an all-out avant-gardist. The more avant-garde a work is, the closer it is to reality for Swerdlow. Since Ionesco's Theatre of the Absurd has been with us many years now, to Stanley it seemed one of the classics, almost on the verge of being dated.

Norman Eisner, the fourth 3W associate with the uncanny knack of pulling projects out of polluted air, did not feel warmly toward *Amédée*. Henry Hoffman, who dug *Hair* on sight, didn't understand *Amédée* at all. Henry and I spent many nights talking about it until, I don't remember when, the play revealed itself to him and he developed a positive passion for it and understood the work better than any of us. Stanley and I managed to put the pieces together, and we had *Amédée* in rehearsals coincident with the *Jacques Brel* previews.

It was bad news from the start. We had a fine young director who had done some very impressive things and a cast of fine players. But nothing jelled. The players as a body didn't seem able to catch the spirit and intelligence of the play. The leading players did not believe in the director, and the two stars hated each other.

Some progress was made, however. In the final rehearsals and previews there were one or two performances of *Amédée* that almost caught fire. Our hopes were strung on yo-yos but the strings were mainly down.

There was a chance we could open *Amédée* and please both critics and audiences. But we were not interested in that sort of crap-game theatre. Our responsibilities as producers involved making final decisions having little to do with audiences and critics; only with ourselves. *Amédée*, in our opinion, had not been properly realized. It did not meet our standards. We heaved a great unorchestrated sigh and closed *Amédée* after its last preview. We had lost $40,000, but we had tried hard.

The *Amédée*'s experience taught me to admire Stan Swerdlow greatly. It was one thing for Henry, Norman, and me to say: "Not good enough." But Stanley had worked for several years to bring *Amédée* to the stage, and he was tearing off a piece of himself when he agreed to close it. A few days later he laughed about it. "I'm keeping my record intact, anyway," he said, "I manage to lose on all the good horses." He was referring to his involvement in the production of LeRoi Jones's *The Slave* and *The Toilet*, and with Megan Terry's *Viet Rock*.

In the end, it was Henry who suggested that we do *Amédée* as a musical. We began to prepare it, and Ionesco heartily agreed.

Meanwhile, *Jacques Brel.*

The first producer, with whom we decided to mount the show, dragged his feet through the summer. After his initial burst of enthusiasm it seemed he had placed the show somewhere on a schedule in the then dim future, for he had other projects both on Broadway and off. He was a good producer, and while I have no doubt that he eventually would have gotten into action, both Mort and I had commitments which required that we must know exactly when *Jacques Brel* would be done. So we withdrew the project.

The next producer combined, we learned, the worst elements a theatre man could have. His tastes were on a very high level but higher still were his fears of the theatre gamble in general. Thus he wanted to be assured of the best players, the best director, the best musicians, etc., while at the same time he would propose a dozen schemes for cutting costs. He thought that one piano might do as well as an orchestra, that two singers could do the work of four, that a young hungry director would contribute his services for credit and the authors should defer their royalties until the investors had recouped their money. By and large my only disagreement with his approach is that it doesn't work.

My 3W associates, in the meantime, were miffed about my not wanting to commit the *Brel* project to the firm. I explained the reasons that prompted me to withhold it. They felt they were invalid. So we auditioned the show for them. 3W became the official producer five minutes after the last song was sung. It was Norman Eisner who asked the dirty question: "How will you stage it? I mean, it's great, but it's theatre, right? So how will you stage it?"

To which I smiled broadly and said, "Norman, that's no problem at all." And I felt like a heel. You see, we trust each other in 3W Productions, Inc.

Interviewing directors only emphasized my fears. Since I had no formal concept to offer, we were subjected to directorial improvisations. Some of the freewheeling ideas of the candidates were not without merit, although totally unrelated to what we wanted. (That is, if I knew what we wanted.) Otis Cavrell came closest to the feeling of what *Brel* should be like on stage, and we agreed that Otis would be our director. But before that could be consummated, Cavrell, a multi-talented man, got an assignment to write a film scenario, and once again we were chasing directors and forms.

Before making decisions about the cast, I was able to convince Mort to play the lead. That scared the hell out of him and everybody else, except Elly Stone who had suggested it. Mort said: "You're out of your bloody skull; I've never performed before." I argued that he'd been performing all his life. He wanted to know: "What will I do with my hands if you take away the piano?" I told him we'd figure it out.

We found a young man by the name of Shawn Elliot who sang well and made a handsome contrast to Mort's big, rugged look. We also cast Alice Whitfield, a small roundish girl with a marvelous blending voice who had spent much of her time as a band singer and a commercial voice-over. With Elly and Mort as the principals we thought we had an ensemble that loooked well and, most important, could sing well. This was not one of those shows where you could choose between actors who could sing badly and singers who could act badly. They had to be able to sing—really sing. Acting was not unimportant but the life of the show absolutely depended on the songs.

After we had cast the original four we looked for two alternates. We got an unexpected break. Bob Guillaume had just returned from Europe where (once again) he had done "Sporting

Life" in *Porgy and Bess*. A handsome, black singer whose tenor voice was beautiful and strong, Guillaume had never won the recognition he easily deserved. Trained for the opera, Bob passed a decade as a night-club singer, folk and pop, group singer, and actor-singer. I had known Bob's work. I had to tell him frankly that he had shown up a few days too late since I had already signed the cast principals. I asked him if he would be willing to learn both male roles and sing for us as an alternate. "I need the bread," he said, and I signed him. When he heard the music later on he told me he really regretted the bad timing of his return to the States. "In a peculiar way," Guillaume said, "there is something black about Brel."

We made a deal with Art D'Lugoff to rent the Village Gate.

Now all we needed was a director and some idea of what in the world we wanted to do with our beautiful bag of songs.

VII

Accidents do play a part. In crap games and in business those who control the game shave the odds against them to a point of reasonable security. In life and in the arts, however, the role of chance is a big one. There is never a hell of a lot of security. You've got to be lucky.

I don't mean that ignorance can help in theatre or any-where else. Yet experience serves only to tell you what may or may not be wrong. Experience takes you only so far, however. You also have to gamble on intuition.

One accident was the Crown of England and the law suit it brought against John Calder and Marion Boyars for publishing *Last Exit to Brooklyn*. The impending trial was regarded as the most important obscenity trial since the *Lady Chatterly* case. John and Marion, being friends of mine, asked me to fly over to London as an expert witness. My background as a slum-reared New Yorker grown to be a writer, they believed, might be important to their defense. This was because part of the prosecution's case rested on the idea that Hubert Selby's book was wholly made up of prurient cloth and thus neither the sights, sounds, situations, nor locations he had described were actually genuine. I could testify toward the validity of those parts of the book. I must confess that the trial did not interest me as much as returning to England and France where I had not been since July, 1945. So I booked a flight.

It was on that crossing, filled with memories of England and France, that I thought of both the form and the director for *Jacques Brel Is Alive and Well and Living in Paris.* The coolness of memory and distance merged with the cry and passion of Brel. Light that never stopped moving. Clarities and depths of lights. Darknesses never totally black. Weighted, flowing movement of players, not dancing but para-natural, the movements being part of memory, thrusting backwards, moving forward into this moment, carrying in the train of motion the changes of mood and texture. Floating; floating. Suddenly descending; rising again. A mobile of sorts.

A mobile in which the text was the songs. The subtext everything else. And the words of Brel culled from unused songs and interviews as a fleeting run of lines to break tensions.

It seemed so real, so whole. The feeling of it was so filled with true colors I knew instantly I wanted to give the project to Moni Yakim to direct. And that was odd because Moni had never directed a musical work, nor had he ever directed spoken theatre. He was a mime.

He was an Israeli mime who had studied under Decroux and Marceau and had played in Marceau's troupe together with his wife Mina. They were now living and performing in the States. Moni had built his own mime theatre from scratch and had trained an entire mime company. It had taken three years. It was a great company—the best I had ever seen. But Yakim's resources gave out, and he could not get enough engagements to support his troupe. He was forced to disband it, and he was destroyed. He told me he felt he had a choice of two things: to kill himself (which was not practical) or to return to Israel where, at least, there would be work for him as an electrician.

My transatlantic vision had been so strong I called Yakim the moment I got into my hotel room. After the preliminary "How are you's?" and "London, you're calling from London? Why are you calling from London?," I laid it out. He was excited and that excitement poured into my ear. It seemed that Yakim not only understood what I had in my head, he also knew Brel's work in the French. Here was another fervent admirer! I assured him I would be back in ten days.

Calder and Boyars picked me up after I had changed clothes. They took me to a pub in John's neighborhood just off Wimpole Street. We talked through the trial problems and the results in the event of a verdict of guilty. The ideological issues were complicated and grave; the monetary issues, in a personal sense, were graver. If they lost, they would be forced into bankruptcy; if they won, they would narrowly avoid bankruptcy. The costs of the legal fight were great.

Even as they explained their dilemma I was impressed by the joy, the absolute joy, with which they faced the trial ahead. Marion was perhaps a shade less joyful than was John, who always enjoyed a good fight. If there was not one at hand, he would surely invent one. (He had been one of the founders and directors of the Edinburgh Festival. One night he wheeled a lovely naked girl across the stage apron in a wheelbarrow in full view of the audience. Quite a scandal. He just felt like shaking those damned people up. He was asked to resign his posts. Being a perfect, if insane, gentleman, he did.)

I told John and Marion about the *Brel* project and John promptly said, "That's a very good idea. And what is Jacques doing these days?"

It was a bit much. Deprived of the pleasure of telling Calder about the significance of Jacques Brel—and how I had discovered him, dammit! I listened half annoyed and half enthralled as John told me about Jacques. He had met him during Brel's first year at Les Trois Baudets. He had visited him frequently then. Yet, strangely, he was not aware of Brel's growth into a major artist. It was on that score that I got my licks in.

I really should not have been surprised that John Calder had sensed Brel's potential so early. After all, it was he who had published the works of Ionesco and Beckett in England. This was usually done prior to the hope of production. So I felt his interest in Brel was a good omen.

There was little time to do anything but be a witness at the trial. The procedure was civilized, which I found amazing since I considered the whole concept of the trial barbaric. The case was lost at Old Bailey and later won on appeal. No one got rich. And in spite of all the fears of the Crown, England was not degraded—not by the free circulation of *Last Exit to Brooklyn,* anyhow.

I went on to Paris for four days. There would be no time to visit the many people I had gotten to know during the war years, among them many of the leading figures in the French Resistance. I decided I wanted to spend all my time with Loys and Paula Masson and walk through the streets of the city. I cannot explain why, but I felt that being on the streets of Paris would bring me closer to Brel's life and work. And it was a good feeling.

Loys Masson was one of the leading poets, playwrights, and novelists of France. The French critics have referred to him as "Our Melville, our Conrad." During the war years he had been second-in-command to Louis Aragon, the poet-novelist who headed the intellectual resistance in the south of France, the so-called Free Zone. Paula had been a resistance courier, often riding her bicycle across the border separating the Free Zone from Occupied France. The Germans sometimes took pot shots at her.

The Massons' apartment on Rue Marcel Renaud was the same one they had found at the end of the war. I had helped them move in, and we had once sat on the floors of the still empty rooms and had drunk wine to celebrate the new place and their good fortune in finding it.

Now it looked old and squalid. The furniture was the same, and the place had not been painted in all that time. At first it had not been painted because Loys had said the place was too small and they would move at the first opportunity. Years passed and it became clear to Paula that they would both never move and never get new paint.

It was grim testimony to the way life had treated them. Loys had worked continuously and had published extensively— something like ten volumes of poetry, a dozen novels, a half dozen plays, many radio and TV dramas. But success brought no rest or security. Loys, when he earned money, was the main support of his family. He had a mother still living in the Mauritian Islands, a painter-brother living in Paris with a large family, and indigent friends, all requiring his support. He gave it and left nothing for himself.

There was no reason for this excepting a deep sense of guilt about many personal things, and especially about the relationship to his family. He also had been deeply hurt by some very close friends who he felt had betrayed him. Between these two pillars of gall his life had degenerated.

Speaking of himself and Paula, still a youthful and beautiful woman in her late forties, he said to me, "We should have died in 1945—that was the year you left us, wasn't it? Life was full then, at its crest. It really had begun to change then, but it took ten years before we could realize it. And then you are too old and too cowardly to do what is necessary."

He was fifty-two, old, sick, and broken. He smoked too much and he drank too much when his health allowed it. He spent most of his hours sleeping in his bedroom-study. He would rise at dawn, dress, and go down the gimpy elevator to walk their tatty little dog. Returning to the apartment, he would work for a few hours before his energies deserted him. Then he would sleep until dinner and retire by nine o'clock.

The fire was out of him. Before coming to France from the Mauritian Islands where he was born, he had been both a shark fisherman and, at 145 pounds, the heavyweight boxing champion.

I remember how at a party given for me and T. S. Eliot (*les deux poètes américains*), Loys had lost control of himself. One never knew how or why his temper would flare.

It began so simply. Masson introduced himself to Eliot and said, "I'm a British citizen. I'm from the Mauritians."

"My dear boy, what you are is a British subject."

"To you, all the niggers begin on the other side of Calais!"

He had said it in complete rage. Yet Eliot, poor man, was only trying to be friendly.

(I should explain that although Masson was white his childhood and adolescence had been spent in intimate friendship with the black people of the Mauritians. He had often told me that he found it more comfortable to think of himself as black. Some of his novels deal with the black experience.)

Paula knew of Brel, but Loys did not. Paula explained to Loys in some detail who Jacques was and reminded him that he had seen and enjoyed Brel in performance. Then Loys remembered but made no comment.

Yet, Brel understood Loys—the dark, tortured, drowning soul of Loys Masson. I wanted so much to play Brel's "Jef" for him or give him the words to read, but I didn't. I spoke seriously only with Paula. With Loys I jollied it up and recounted the old days, the good times. Once or twice I got him to laugh. It occurred to me later that I was almost acting out the theme of "Jef." Actually, it was Paula who was acting that theme; she had done it for two decades.

(Masson was dying—it was that simple. He was dying because he wanted to die. It finally happened two years later. He was to meet Paula, who was staying in the countryside, but never showed up. They found him with his coat on, sitting bolt upright on the one chair in the kitchen. He had wrapped up the garbage to take out; it was one of the few household tasks he had assumed.

He died on the day I had arrived in Paris for a meeting with Mort and Jacques. I told them of Masson's passing. I must have been upset because they were both silent. Then Jacques sighed. We ordered drinks and went on with our lives.)

The visit with the Massons had been very depressing. I hoped at the time that Loy's spirits had been somewhat revived by my unyielding optimism. I committed a foolish and sentimental act when I gave Loys my good luck piece, a gold spatula I carried in my breast pocket. I assured him that it would bring him the same good luck it had brought me. It didn't do him a bit of good; it had never done me any good either.

In addition to acquiring Yakim I was delighted to get Lily Turner to come aboard as our general manager. Aside from being one of the people who was a charter founder of Off-Broadway theatre, Lily is one of the few consummate professionals operating within the amateur night we call theatre. She put our understructure smoothly together and guided us away from the thousand traps theatre producers are often heir to.

Lily also brought us James Nisbet Clark, who designed our lighting and stage-managed the show. Jim is a barrelful of theatre trades: an actor, stage designer, light designer, director, writer, and artist. I do not know him in all of these capacities, but as a light designer he is superb. It is not even fair to say he is simply a light designer; he literally grows light designs. They emerge, emerge, and emerge until finally you say, "My God, that's beautiful!" Yet, because his designs are almost biologically evolved to support and interpret the endless shifting surfaces of the *Brel* show, Jim wound up with more than 200 light cues. A fearful number of light changes; few people have attempted as many. He also worked for a couple of months to formalize his concept and put it on paper as our official light plot.

Mort discovered Wolfgang Knittel. Wolf is a German-born, classically trained pianist, composer, and conductor. But in spirit and by choice he is a jazz man. Wolf arranged the music under Mort's general musical direction. The approach Knittel used was right on. He preserved the French feeling, and yet had made the complete sound something that was American. This was accomplished by refusing to use the tell-tale accordian and by including an electric guitar, fender bass, and electric mandolin in the orchestra, where the four musicians doubled and tripled in the combination of electric and accoustical sounds.

I hired Ivan Black for our press relations. It seems I always hire Ivan Black. It's not because I prefer Harvard men on the team or because Ivan is the greatest publicist in show business. (He's one of the best, though.) I just feel good when Ivan is around. He's in his late sixties, and through Ivan I feel connected with a great span of theatrical history. Also he is a kind of ideal— a physical bull who exudes energy as if he were Con Ed in a good year without pollution. A good man, trained as an architect, who fell into the *boîtes* of make believe.

So we were all put together, and on December 9, 1967, we descended into the basement of the Village Gate and started to rehearse.

VIII

The last smash hit that played Art D'Lugoff's cockamamie theatre was *MacBird*. And even before we were ten minutes into rehearsal down in his vasty cellar, he was assuring me that I would be a smash hit too. I know how to pick them, he said. Then like Alice's White Rabbit in full black beard, D'Lugoff rolled away into one of the many holes which make the Village Gate so mysterious.

The Village Gate, probably the world's most important jazz center, is situated in what were once the cafeterias and the laundry rooms of the old Mills Hotel, now called the Greenwich Hotel. Then, as now, it was a flophouse.

The building had been designed by the eminent and infamous Stanford White with an emphasis on function that was not to exclude certain elements of elegance and culture. The socially inspired purpose for the Mills was to offer a place, both clean and inexpensive, to upright American youths who found themselves hard up in New York—an oasis in the wilderness of the wicked city. Inside the building somewhere there is, I am told, a first-class theatre that is never used. I have never seen it myself, mainly because I'm not brave enough to go into the hotel.

The plans for the old Mills as a social institution never quite worked out. The twenty-five-cent-a-night room rent mainly attracted the lumpens, the winos, and the junkies. Today, the rate has soared to a dollar fifty, but the clientele remains much the same. The most notable difference is that most of the gents at the hotel are paid by government agencies, and it is commonplace to see welfare and pension checks delivered in quantity.

The one notable change in the Mills-Greenwich is the establishment of the Village Gate, and the hotel above it tries very hard to reject it, knowing it is an alien transplant. One must be alert for the occasional bottle that flies down. But better that than to be caught in one of the alleyways and pissed upon. The Village Gate might be an offstage locale of *The Three-Penny Opera,* and in that sense a near-perfect place to present *Jacques Brel Is Alive and Well and Living in Paris.*

The Village Gate Theatre is actually a nightclub that permitted us to design our show as "cabaret theatre," a term that clearly defines itself. There is a stage area and set before or around its perimeter are tables and chairs where you may drink or smoke. The main advantages of cabaret theatre are the intimacy created without illusion and the sense of reality, of being in a real place, where audience is as vulnerable as actor. Proscenium theatre separates the play from the audience and tends to make the auditors nonparticipants and, in a certain sense, *voyeurs.* The voyeuristic sense, however, is always diminished because the play is done *now* by living people. Film carries the separation of the doers and the watchers to the maximum degree in spite of its supersized images. Yet no matter what the spatial and emotional relationships are between medium and audience, the task of finally merging the audience with the stage or film play is much the same and the measure, I believe, of its artistic success.

The preconceptions of the producers, writers and director are only the rough first sketches that establish a time, a place, and direction wherein we hopefully will find that essential play life held foggily in our separate heads. It is what we perceive as we build the work that counts. From the moment the players are on the stage and the words in their mouths all preconceptions modify in favor of new actualities. The bodies of the players, their voices, and their psychological makeup already contribute toward changing the weights and colors of our preconceptions. These onstage verities develop opportunities for the director to discover what factors he is really manipulating and how it all affects the work at hand.

However, what evolves must not fall into improvisation, no

matter how much arises from that source. It has always seemed perfectly ludicrous to me to have a work suddenly remade because of cast qualities and directorial adventure. I hold very closely to the idea of a writer's theatre and cast a baleful eye at directors who mistake themselves for writers or prime creators. Of course, there may be some redoing on everyone's part, including that of the author, to make the play work. Yet he must be a very poor writer whose work must be completely changed to make it valid somehow. Good writers are always closer to the final play evolved. Otherwise who needs them?

From the day we began to rehearse we were not far from the final *Brel*. Our main problems concerned which songs to sing and in which order. However, we knew what we wanted: to order the songs and their interpretation in such a way as to create the theatre experience as opposed to the concert or variety experience. To reveal our characters, who in one way or another represented the feelings and ideas of Brel and, in part, Brel himself, as people who were caught in the dark human comedy and who were unwilling, in spite of all they had experienced, to abandon either the joy or hope that makes life bearable. Through trial and error we tested our work against that goal and, give or take an ambivalence or two, we reached that goal.

The result was a "librettoless musical." Its form was neither musical comedy nor revue. It was a special form of musical theatre. Many productions have used our approach, some successfully and some unsuccessfully. Yet, in my own mind, I do not think that our little theatre of song has any but the most limited of formal values. What it does is to replace spoken text by song text —scarcely startling. Its particular validity was our recognition that Brel had given us the scenes and minidramas in the songs themselves, and "librettoless" was the correct way to use them. At one point I had thought our theatre of song was quite original, but I was disabused when an Indian director, visiting the show, told me enthusiastically he was so happy to see American theatre using an Indian theatrical form. He then described a form of Indian theatre not very different from our *Brel*, except that it had been used in India for more than fifteen hundred years!

Somewhere during the rehearsal period we auditioned the show for Columbia Records. It was a gala little event. Almost all of the brass crowded into the little audition room to check out the burgeoning "inside" rumors about this *Brel* work.

Elly Stone tinkled the keys of the piano and said to me *sotto voce:* "Isn't it typical? Big company. Wall to wall carpets. Good middlebrow decor. Built-in bar with good booze. And a lousy spinet piano out of tune—naturally!"

But Wolf Knittel played it anyway, and our mighty little cast blew the minds of the Columbia general staff. Thus we got our recording contract. (Subsequently, the two-record album of the show became one of the all-time best sellers in that category.) The Columbia people thought it the best audition they had heard in years.

Ironically, when the initial poor reviews for *Brel* appeared, the Columbia enthusiasts promptly suggested we forgo the advance we were to be paid under the terms of the contract. That made me furious, and I refused to hear of it. It had nothing to do with the money involved. 3W had several times offered to split the cost of full-page ads with Columbia and other promotional items like that. This approach was always too damned expensive for Columbia. Our attitudes differed. Theirs was: business is business; mine was: principle is principle. I really cannot suggest seriously that my view is the better of the two. It may make you feel good, but you will usually wind up the loser. I prefer feeling good—a serious aberration.

At one point during rehearsals we got a real scare. Mort Shuman's voice was about to vanish. Untrained as a singer, he was on the verge of destroying his voice. Here, as she was to do on so many occasions, Lillian Strongin dashed onto the scene to save us.

What can I offer to Lillian Strongin other than total praise, adulation, and love? She was perhaps the greatest artist among us. I am convinced that no one in the world knows the human voice better than she, no one better understands the process of singing or more fully understands the beauty to be brought forth from the human voice. I cannot describe her as a singing teacher merely because she does that so well. She is one of the rare guardians of the beauty of singing. It is no accident that the works of Giovanni Lamperti are in her charge as continuor and executrix. (Lamperti was one of the greatest teachers and exponents of *bel canto* singing the world has ever known and Lillian struggles to keep Lamperti's sound ringing in the spoiled world of song.) Elly Stone is one of her pupils and Lillian fully expects Elly to take over for her when she retires. She is sixty-seven now, but I think she will be here decades after I'm gone.

Lillian took Mort and slapped his ass around the block, but she saved and repaired his voice and gave him insights into what real singing was. Subsequently, she aided other singers in the show, and many of these she disliked both as singers and as performers. She did the necessary tinkering, however, to make sure that *Brel* continued for she, like all of us, had fallen in love with Brel's marvelous songs. Some day I would love to have her meet Jacques and have him listen to her extraordinary critique of his work as his songs relate to pure singing. I would give a lot to witness that exposition.

Yakim found the style that beautifully fitted the form. Clark grew his bouquets of light. Sometimes, what happened was very beautiful, strong, and moving. Elly in those rehearsal days was at times so heartrending that Yakim spoke again in suicidal tones. And all of us, bundled in our sweaters in the drafty cold cellar, trembled above the frost at those exquisite moments of making our play come alive. For what is rehearsing if not making love? Finding new ways to kiss, to touch, to enter, to complete.

But the point arrives too soon when we have explored all of the ways of love, and then, of a sudden, we one day realize that Our Lady of Light and Shadow has conceived. We are thrilled and frightened by that. Her belly is full, and the months are gone, and we have nothing left but to have our baby.

That happens on opening night.

Like so many others in the theatre, I find opening nights an abominable practice.

However, *Jacques Brel* and we were ready to meet audience and critic in an official sense. The previews had gone exceedingly well and had given us the opportunity to make a few final cuts and adjustments. We cut "Caramels" (our version of "Les Bonbons") because it was the one lyric we could not make work well enough without its being an insult to the original. We also eliminated "Flatlands" ("Le Plat Pays"), which was extraordinarily beautiful, because our sense of invention failed us. It was slow, stately, grand, and intense, but we could not decide on how to stage it and where to place it. Time bore down on us heavily. So with great regret we scratched "Flatlands." I have never been without a pang in my belly when I think of that woeful amputation, especially since I have never been able to convince myself that we had done the right thing.

So we had our baby. To the parents it was born radiant, and we accepted the cheers and adulation of the audience as being completely right, absolutely justified.

But the critics, hearing the cheers and the applause at the birth of the child, always conclude that opening nights are family affairs and that all of the loud enthusiasm is merely dutiful.

I am told that critics very often turn off a play when the audience turns on too high. I suspect this is partly true because I have been often cautioned by Ivan Black to hold down my applause and bravos at performances of *Brel* because the critic from East Merde was in the house. "But they are doing a beautiful show!," I would say between a whistle and a bravo.

"He'll think that you are a claque."

"But look at the others! They are louder than I am. Look over there; they are on their feet screaming."

"But we can't control them. You should have more sense. The East Merde critic is very important."

"Tell him to go fuck himself."

On opening night, however, I made not a sound. I just drank myself into the necessary oblivion and did, for me, what comes closest to praying. I talked to myself.

It is true that on opening night the audience behaved like a great beast, ecstatically full of orgiastic bellows, snorts, and charges of applause and bravos. But as more than a half million people, who have now seen the Brel show, know that is exactly how our audiences have always reacted. If only I had known them, I would have bound and gagged those stupid, tasteless bastards who bought tickets and made such an ungodly scene on opening night!

The reviewers for the *The New York Times* and the *New York Post* clobbered us. Poor Dan Sullivan and poor Jerry Tallmer, both bright men for whom I have an uncommon regard and respect, had missed it all. They seemed neither to see nor hear that night.

I take comfort in the fact, and I ask them to do the same,

that this sort of at-the-event myopia has many precedents. One can check the files of *The New York Times* and read, for example, what one reviewer had to say about Herman Melville's *Moby Dick*. Something like: "Burn it, baby, burn it!"

The negative and inadvertently insulting reviews by Tallmer and Sullivan were not so bad as the attitudes of some of the others. Many critics did not bother to attend because they could not imagine what the show might be other than a night club act, hardly worthy of their bodies and minds. One critic, hallowed be her name, squirmed in her panty hose and decided that *Jacques Brel* was not even worth panning in print.

But others felt good about the work, and I was more than gratified to find that both Julius Novick of *The Village Voice* and James Davis of the *Daily News* shared our enthusiasm for *Jacques Brel*.

Vanity and personal feelings to one side, it is a bloody hard fact that you cannot survive without a strong review from *The New York Times*. All of the rest practically do not matter. That's how it's been since the passing of the *New York Herald-Tribune*.

I talked with the cast and our director, musicians, and technical people and told them I was thankful for all their good work and we had accomplished what we had set out to do. I was satisfied and had no regrets, but I had no great hopes we could survive.

However, there were two people and one development I could not foresee. It developed that the preview audiences had been very busy doing their thing, which is called "word-of-mouth." Audiences mysteriously began to arrive in numbers not quite large enough to allow us to carry the show yet significant "because they had heard." Weekday audiences roared up to as many as fifty, and on weekends they often passed a hundred. We needed about 170 people at each of the eight performances to break even. But those who came were sending others, and I would hover at the box-office window of a Tuesday night and smile when we had broken eighty ticket sales. There was motion, certainly, but I could not see it as being fast enough. We would have to go down.

However, there was Henry Hoffman. He stood with me at every single performance during those first weeks after the reviews, shaking his head in disbelief and often being moved to tears by the performances. Stanley Swerdlow's reaction was the same.

"We can't close this show. How can we possibly close this show? It's too beautiful."

"Henry, we have got to close it. We are losing about two thousand dollars a week. Let's not be unprofessional. We can't make money this way."

"If I wanted to make money, I wouldn't go into theatre. I know all about making money. Do you want to close it?"

"We *have* to close it."

"I didn't ask you if we have to close it. I asked if you *want* to close it."

"No."

"Then we'll keep it open."

"How long? You're just extending the agony; how long?"

"For a year if necessary."

"You're out of your freaky mind. Why?"

"Look Eric, it's like a middle-aged guy having an eighteen-year-old mistress. You know she's going to cost you a lot of money, and she can't do you any good, but as long as she's there you've got to have her."

So Henry gave the audiences a chance to come to us, and the word moved around.

Apparently, the word came to Clive Barnes of *The New York Times*. Barnes showed up for a Sunday matinee. It was not so much that he gave us a fantastic review—one that went a long way toward allowing us to sell the show and move it from red to black and finally to profit—that makes me remember Clive Barnes with warmth. It was that he rose to his feet and applauded the show with the rest of the audience. He was not just the senior reviewer of *The New York Times;* he was a human being and *Jacques Brel* had gotten to him, and he had the grace not to deny it.

Our story had a happy ending.

IX

Since then, I have wondered what it is that theatre criticism is supposed to be and what theatre critics are supposed to do. I'm talking about the pop critics—those who cover theatre for newspapers and large-circulation magazines.

Indeed, I question whether newspaper reviewers have a proper function, i.e. that they are really critics of theatre. I think most such reviewers are, at best, reporters of the news that emanates from the theatre world, including their instant report on the play opening of the night before.

Few theatre writers are as well equipped for their jobs as, let us say, sports writers. A baseball writer knows the field he covers quite intimately. He knows its history. He knows the playing field dimensionally and the purpose and effect of field dimensions in both their blueprint sense and in the ways they vary under actual circumstances. He can evaluate the roll of the ground along the foul lines and the role prevailing winds will play during the course of the game. He knows in detail and can evaluate the functions of the management, the trainers, the umpires, and the athletes in the play of the game.

It is also imperative that sports writers have a total grasp of the game because sports audiences are pretty sophisticated and can easily spot ignorance in a journalist. On TV and radio it has become commonplace to have former professional athletes take over some of the on-the-air coverage, and the general commentator readily defers to the precise observations of his ex-athlete associate. Obviously, there is no comparison between theatre and sports and little comparison between sports writers and theatre writers. It is the decomparison that I find useful. Baseball is only a game—a matter of form and execution—and those who comment on it are concerned only with competitive skills and the final outcome.

Theatre is not a game. It is an art most often concerned with and reflective of the world in which we live. It comprises perhaps ten or twelve craft skills that can be individually evaluated and have as their combined purpose the achievement of art.

Based on our experience with the *Brel* show I suspect that very few reviewers have the skills required to evaluate what they see on the stage. Sometimes they are skillful and entertaining *writers,* but rarely critics, critique makers, or aestheticians. They are, alas, glamorized members of the audience not very different from the general ticket buyer, except that they are in a position to broadcast their opinions to innumerable readers and viewers.

Why? I think it is that through the years theatre has slowly come to rest on the borderline fronting the more popular arts—movies and TV. Dance, opera, and mime being far less popular arts in the United States develop smaller, more sophisticated audiences complete with open snobbery and critics who support that snobbery. These arts belong to special groups and have small general appeal. Patrons, subscribers, and foundations pay the bills, and the same audiences return again and again to their private enthusiasms. In these areas the critics and patrons share a special view. The critics are technically better equipped, but their purpose seems to exclude new audiences or new artistic growth.

The general theatre reviewer on the other hand wants everybody to attend theatre! Most theatre in New York is unsubsidized, and New York, like it or not, is the heart of theatre. It is bitterly competitive. Its life depends on the sale of high-priced tickets, and the crazy group of investors who never tire of betting long shots.

These circumstances develop producers who mount works *designed* to sell tickets. So they bend theatre content toward TV and movie standards, and the critics soon develop a mote in their eye: they see themselves as benign manipulators with a duty to "keep theatre alive," by helping the producer to sell tickets to plays that are not much more than live TV shows. Hence so many marvelous reviews for shows that are in reality quite poor. Here I do not mean cheap, silly, etc; I mean no matter what they are doing they do it so badly that audiences—even those who want almost TV-theatre—do not like it. For in the end the audiences do make the final judgment in the war between themselves and ad quotes, promotion, and publicity. It is audiences that produce new audiences for plays they like or convince potential audiences to stay away from plays they do not like. Word-of-mouth finally rules.

I believe that, and in believing it I do not try to read an

audience's mind. I do not know what that might be. I make it simpler. I do my production and I invite the audiences to read *my* mind. If they dig me I am in; if they dig me not I am done.

What I ask of the critic is to understand better than he does now what he is looking at, and write that down. To hell with saving theatre in general; save only the good play (good to you, personally, dear fellow; Aunt Mathilda in Dubuque is a secret drinker, anyhow). What else does a critic have but his acquired knowledge, intuition and, I hope, his sense and need to express his personal viewpoint?

Reviewers are not to be blamed for this situation. They did not create it. They simply found their employment there rather than on the police beat or on the foreign desk. And it is a pleasant assignment, for it brings prestige and power and your opinion does count for something. Therefore, all theatre writers, try to learn something about theatre! It does not take too much time before one can talk and write about it as if one had invented it. Not so different from psychoanalytic highballing, but vastly different from sports or science.

And by the way, what exactly is Theatre?

I ask that question because while there were reviewers who had no doubts we had created *theatre,* there were some, loving us just as much, who thought that perhaps we were a night-club act. Was *Jacques Brel Is Alive and Well and Living in Paris* truly theatre or was it actually a club act done inside a place called a theatre and given superficial theatre trappings?

There are neither standard definitions nor standard feelings to describe theatre. Aside from dictionary definitions, I do not know of a work or a body of work that satisfactorily describes theatre either as a physical entity or as an art entity.

It is somewhat easier to define Music, or Painting, or Dance, or Writing. In these areas we are not only surer of the nature of the discipline, but we are more adventurous in our acceptance of range and variety. But in theatre, where we combine and use all these elements and more, we are less sure, less tolerant, and less simple. Film, which is somewhat more technical and complicated as a composite of almost all arts, does not prevent us from completely identifying it. No matter what is put on it, Agnew or Hamlet, a motion picture is a motion picture.

But what is put on a stage is not necessarily theatre. And that makes for the rub and wide gash in critical responses.

I cannot offer a definition of theatre. Like most others I do not know what it is, nor am I very sure of what it is not. My only guide is that I have seen a good deal of theatre and have tried to create some of it, and thus I am able, like others, to recognize it. In short, I know it when I see it.

In a physical sense one can create theatre almost anywhere —not merely in a formal area behind a proscenium, or at the bottom of the bowl of an arena theatre either indoors or out, on unmasked and open platforms, or on thrusting platforms, but, if you like, in a cornfield, or a village square, or on the gundeck of a battleship, or in the auditorium of P.S. 64, or at the Copacabana, Where have theatre players not performed plays?

But what do they perform that makes us say: this is theatre? Most often it is the words of writers who have created scenes and actions to entertain an audience. Sometimes they combine songs and dances with a libretto, and we call that musical theatre. Once we called it musical comedy, before the idea struck us that more serious themes could be handled in that form. In musical theatre we now do not hesitate to eliminate the chorus line leaving only libretto and music and song. We can opt for other eliminations as well without, I think, losing the fact that we are still presenting and dealing with theatre.

If we sing the entire libretto and change the nature of the music, we have traditional opera, which is slowly yielding to more contemporary approaches. Is opera theatre? Is operetta theatre? Clearly, yes.

If we throw out libretto and song and go with music and dance we can have Dance Theatre. Of course, libretto, song, and dance can be eliminated and music reduced to a background function, leaving us only with bodily movement, and thus we could have Mime Theatre. And eliminate people on the stage and have Puppet and Marionette Theatre, etc.

I do not think, however, that night-club acts are theatre, although they sometimes may be theatrical. Nor is variety. Nor standard burlesque. Nor an entertainer who does a one-man singing show. Yet there can be a one-man show that does achieve theatre.

The pertinent difference, it seems to me, is that in all theatre we are presented with a more-or-less total ambiance, a special sense of time and place, through which the action moves and which, at its best, involves us as the audience in a special world with special experiences to which we are forced to relate. We become engaged, and we have come to that world, the theatre, precisely because we wanted to be engaged in the first place. It is my conviction that we *feel* theatre, we *smell it out,* without actually defining it.

In *Jacques Brel* our single shift in emphasis was the elimination of the spoken text in musical theatre. The show was no less theatre because of that. (I have just laughed suddenly because I remember the round man poking his cigar into the face of his companion and vehemently protesting: "Yeah, but what's the plot?")

The fact that theatre journalists can sometimes fail to recognize theatre when it slightly shifts its working elements is not so bad. Yet even when they are dealing with standard theatre— theatre they can recognize—they seem unable to evaluate it constructively. They seem able only to tell us that they liked it or disliked it.

A play is presented, and the critics do not like the presentation. Was the play badly written or was it a good play badly directed and badly performed?

Another play is presented, and the critics like it. Was the play a good one, or was it a *tour de force* achieved by director and actors?

Theatre journalism largely avoids these questions, but genuine criticism begins with such questions. What is required always is an evaluation of the total work and how its parts function in relation to the whole.

Such a total evaluation presupposes the relationship of the particular work to the particular time in a particular society that has deeply influenced its form and style. (This may give us a clue as to why badly played Shakespeare is horrendous to watch while a contemporary work done equally badly sometimes seems palatable.) Directly or indirectly, therefore, we are asking critics to understand the world in which the play is presented and in which the critic lives, and that is a lot to ask of anyone. Yet, it must be asked in the hope of developing great critics.

The evaluation of elemental parts of a theatre work requires a good working knowledge on the part of the critic, and such knowledge is acquired through hard work. The critic must learn to *evaluate*, and the more tools the critic possesses the better his evaluation will be. Like anyone else in theatre, the critic must have talent.

In the evaluation of the Brel show, I found only one writer really equipped to deal with the translations. He was Rudel-Tessier of *La Presse* in Montreal. In the first place, Tessier was bilingual. In the second place, he knew the works of Jacques Brel, and he had often heard Brel perform. In the third place, Tessier was keenly aware of technical problems of making such translations of poems and lyrics. He is a rare one, Tessier.

There is a beautiful irony here. We played the show in Montreal, and we were slaughtered by the English-language newspapers in that city. The writers were white with rage. We, in their view, were killing Jacques Brel, and we had committed sacrilege by daring to translate him at all. (Brel is a great hero in French Canada.)

Rudel-Tessier, on the other hand, thought that we had done a noble job in our translations. He pointed out that we had transmogrified Jacques Brel, and Brel had become a sort of "James Brel" processed through the filters of a New York–U.S.A. experience.

Tessier was able to clarify and evaluate our translations for his readers by comparing a line of English to a line of French, or a text in French to a text in English. He thought we were fine in English, but obviously we had put a good deal of ourselves into the work, and some of Jacques Brel had gone out of the work. (True.) Yet, Tessier went on, it was still Brel and marvelous to have him in English in this form. He chided his readers a bit and asked them to be happy that Shakespeare is in French although it is not the same as Shakespeare in English.

In two talks with Tessier I had the opportunity to explore many areas of the art of translation.

I believe it is totally impossible to translate a poem line or a song-text line word for word and preserve the music and grace of the poem or, in the case of the song text, the grace, feeling, and music-fit. In such a literal translation one may even lose the very meaning of the original. It is perhaps comparable to having a child's drawing of a house. It is nothing at all like the object it represents, but we can recognize it when we happen to know the object the drawing has tried to depict. In poems and song texts much of the meaning is inextricably bound to word sound and word movement.

In translating a song text one must know and feel what it says. My own approach, when I am satisfied that I know what the text is about, is to attempt to stay close to original words and images.

But since a song text is not a crossword puzzle, knowing all of the words in each language involved is hardly enough to transform a song from one language to another. Sometimes the English words are alien to the sound of the French words, and the song will die, for so much of a song text is vital because of the way it sounds. Thus, a translated word-equivalent must have the sound to go with it if there is a chance of realizing the original gut feeling.

It is the *sound* feeling that I try to grasp first. Then I search for the feeling of sense through the sound combined with the original word meaning and embodied image. If these two elements fall in place, the translation will move along well and stay close to the original.

But should the English words lack the sounds of the French, there is little chance to stay close to the sensual nature of the images, for these are spelled out in word-terms in the first place. When this happens, we find ourselves at one remove from the original text, and we are now faced with the problem of adaptation rather than translation per se, although there is always some adaptation even in close translations.

Since it is the job of the adaptation to hold onto the essence —the spirit—of the original, I find that capturing the original sound quality is more important than holding onto the images in the song text. Should one decide to use new sets of images (and I have frequently), the battle is to find new images that do not contradict the sense or sound of the original. (In "La Valse à mille temps" the waltz image is replaced by wheels, and the song becomes "Carousels." In "Jef" the desperation of two drunks trying to re-establish their lives is replaced by the desperation of two lovers, and becomes "No Love You're Not Alone.")

Sometimes I have chosen to adapt because the cultural gap seemed to make a close translation invalid in terms of our American culture. (This path was followed in "Jef.")

Translation or adaptation, the process remains a delicate one. I have settled for the idea that a good part of the process has to do with catching the essential spirit of the man behind the work. The better I understood Brel as a creator, and the closer I felt to his life in art, the greater became my chance of bringing him into English and into American psychological and cultural terms that kept Brel as much Brel as he possibly could be made. Thus the French Brel became the American Brel, became *our* Brel.

Since translation is an act of tarnishing, those making translations are deeply pleased when the original remains alive and is not a ghost of its former self. Every translation is a harmful act; like a surgeon cutting into a living body, there will always be a scar of some kind. There will always be the knowledge that had life been different the operation might not have been necessary at all.

I have dwelt on the matter of translation because it shows, aside from my belief that Rudel-Tessier is a good critic, that a good critic can give much to theatre people through genuine evaluation. Tessier makes one think and rethink one's work both in general and specific terms.

Jacques Brel has received wonderfully generous reviews from quick critics both inside and outside the United States. This has given me a noncarping platform to examine some of the problems in theatre reviewing and criticism. Moreover, the tribe of theatre writers is a good one, made up mainly of gentlemen who are bright and can be generous beyond belief.

It is difficult to be simple. It is difficult to be true. It is difficult to enjoy our lives and the dominant functions within our lives. Worst of all, perhaps, is that the establishment doesn't care very much for critics of theatre; they are too insignificant. It is only the theatre audience, the actor, the writer, the producer, etc., to whom the critic is of inordinate importance.

But we all want better theatre; we all want better critics. Great ones if we can have them. Not mere journalistic entertainers.

X

Everything was beautiful in the spring of 1968. It was not just that we had won all our bets, but that we had won those bets on our terms.

It meant something to see our players sulk when they had not done a performance up to standard. It meant something to see Melina Mercouri weeping as she watched us do the show. She returned eight or ten times, and on each visit she had a large party in tow. When we offered her complimentary tickets she reared up in all her Greek majesty and said: "I pay! You give me all of this (her arm knifing toward the stage), I pay!" And Melina knew Brel's work. She owned all of his records. It was good to have her with us as a friend.

It meant something to have Marcel Marceau there talking his head off and explaining what we had done, or to have Angela Lansberry come backstage blowing her nose and saying to Elly Stone: "I am at your feet!"

It was also marvelous to have Donald Pleasance come to *Jacques Brel* on Sunday nights when his show, *Man in the Glass Booth* was dark. He sat ringside, his bald head gleaming, his cheeks rivered with tears.

And how touching it was to learn that synagogues and churches were using some of the Brel songs in formal and informal ceremonies, and to have The Bible Society use "If We Only Have Love" as the official song of National Bible Week, and to hear peace marchers singing the same song.

Still I felt an emptiness. I wanted Jacques to see the show, and I would bug Mort about it. "Call him. Call him. When will he be here?"

Mort did call, and he wrote. At first, Jacques thought he might come in March, then in April. Then there was a movie to do; and then some recording; then *La Mancha.* I gave up on the hope that he would come at all.

But Madame Brel came that spring. Her being there gave me more jitters than did opening night. Miche knew English quite well, and who could question her knowledge of Jacques' songs?

I was introduced to Miche by Mort before the show. It was a very stiff and formal meeting—proper smiles, proper enthusiasm, very proper manners from each of us. At that moment of introduction (I realized later) my own insecurity prevented me from noting Miche's own extreme anxiety.

The curtain went up for her, and I watched from the side. She barely moved; her face was frozen. She applauded mechanically, and my heart withered. After all, if we had failed for her, would we not also fail for Jacques?

After the performance, still frozen, Miche told me how pleased she was. She went backstage and told the cast how good they all were. Her speech was clipped, her back stiff. We were all convinced that she had hated it. For the first time, I actually thought we might have failed.

But Miche returned the next night. We had not expected her. Now she was completely relaxed. She was gay; her laughter was genuine and easy. The grip of her hand was alive. And she carried bouquets of flowers for Elly Stone. I didn't know what to make of it, but it felt good. She laughed and cried. Her face was bright. I came to her at the end as she sat beaming at the empty stage.

I almost accused her: "So you *did* like it!"

Her head bobbed rapidly. "It is marvelous! Marvelous!"

"We all thought you were unhappy with it. We felt terrible."

"Oh, no, no. I'm sorry. I was so frightened. I didn't know how it would be. I was paralyzed. Is that the right word? I went to my hotel after, and I cried I was so happy."

She was still seated on the straight-backed chair that comes with your ticket to the *Brel* show at the Gate, and I squatted before her. Quite suddenly she said to me, "Which do you think are Jacques' most important songs?"

And although neither one was in the show, I answered without hesitating, " 'Plat Pays' and 'Mon Enfance.' "

Her head nodded rapidly: "Will you translate them?"

"I have already done 'Plat Pays' and I certainly intend to do 'Mon Enfance.' " (I did translate "My Childhood" soon after that, and Elly Stone recorded it on her remarkable Columbia Records album.)

Miche remained in New York for a week. She came to see

the show another time. I asked her when Jacques would come, and she said she didn't know; she thought he, like herself, was afraid to see what we had done.

So the time passed. We spread out. London. Chicago. Toronto. Philadelphia. Washington. Palm Beach. Los Angeles. San Francisco. Boston. Tours and one-nighters. And no matter where we went people were moved by Brel.

Even in Palm Beach where the elderly descendants of the "robber barons" live, we moved them. Not in the way we expected, but we moved them all the same.

We had been warned, when we accepted the engagement, that the Palm Beach opening-night audience was not to be believed for its *hauteur,* rudeness, and utter boredom. A few weeks earlier the manager of the theatre had taken a full-page ad in the newspapers excoriating his patrons for their unbelievable conduct when they had attended a performance of *Rosencrantz and Guildenstern Are Dead.* And now, along came *Jacques Brel.*

On opening night I stood outside the Royal Poinciana Playhouse and watched an amazing exhibition. The Bentleys and the Rolls Royces hissed gently down the palm-lined avenue. Chauffeurs leaped out to open doors. Patrons stepped out on unsteady feet. Great cartoons in color: George Grosz. Couturier gowns. Diamond tiaras. Gentlemen in burnished evening clothes. All already slightly tipsy. Daintily they made their way along the infinite red carpet, past the TV camera men, more puppets than peacocks, and then into the theatre to the waiting bar. They had displayed and they had been seen, and they were now waiting for us to perform.

Minute by minute they hated us. When John C. Attle on his stage-right platform finished singing "Statue" all hell broke loose. A man in a red dinner jacket, his face matching it, leaped up from his seat. "You sons of bitches," he cried, "you dirty bastards!"

Then others responded to his wild shout, and the air bristled with "bastards" and "bitches." Programs were flung onto the stage, and more than half the audience, shouting and muttering, noisily walked out.

On stage, Mort whispered to Elly: "The enemy has declared himself," and, quite appropriately, the cast was singing "The Desperate Ones."

As an aftermath we were asked to censor the show. We politely declined and played through our week. We were delighted to find the young people, college students, and the churches strongly in our support and buying up all the tickets turned in by those we had offended. It's certain that *Jacques Brel* didn't bore anybody.

In the fall of 1969, during our visit with Jacques, I made him solemnly promise to see our show. He came in November. I felt no anxiety this time; Jacques would approve. I knew this so deeply I could not wait for the night to come. While waiting for *the* night, I spent the afternoon with him.

I picked him up at his hotel. How tired he was! As tired as the first night I had met him after his concert in Carnegie Hall. His hair needed trimming, and the lines in his face somehow seemed deeper. Yet it was only a month since I had seen him in Paris. I think he knew that I was noticing these things, and he seemed to straighten up in response.

He spoke first: "How are you, you are well? My English is improving. My name is Jacques Brel. You are Eric Blau, I presume?"

But his English had not improved that much, and soon we were back into our French-English, English-French patois. It worked better this time. Probably because we had no one with us to translate.

I had assured Jacques that we would not use his visit for publicity purposes. We had taken great pains to fend off newspapers, magazines, columnists, and TV shows. People knew he was in New York because Air France had issued a bulletin announcing his arrival. So I had to deal with the nice guys and the nasty ones. The nice ones were content with the truth: he was not up to interviews; he had come to New York to relax and write a little. The nasty ones were content with nothing.

"Do you mean to say that you will not tell me where he is staying?"

"I do not know where he is staying."

"I can find out myself, you know."

"OK. Find out."

"You're not very cooperative. We can be uncooperative, too."

"I am aware of that."

"Well?"

"Kiss my ass."

"What?"

"Kiss my ass."

"OK, wise guy."

Click. Click.

Moving through the city with Jacques was not at all like trying to be incognito with Jackie Onassis. The odds that he would be recognized by anyone but a Belgian or Frenchman were astronomical. I knew it and he knew it.

I suggested the Stage Delicatessen because it was very "New York." We walked crosstown toward it. Jacques bundled and hunched into the light wind and complained that he was cold. He skipped along the sidewalk in little bursts getting ahead of me and then waited for me to catch up.

When we sat down in the Stage I asked him if there was anything wrong, if he felt all right. He smiled that strange, charming, boyish, very wise smile and said that he was bone tired. He didn't know why except, and it was hard to admit it to himself, that he was feeling his age. He couldn't burn his life the way he once did— not that he didn't want to—it just wouldn't go. He couldn't sit with a bottle of whisky before him and drink with no debilitating results. A few drinks and he would become depressed and weary. Everything was becoming more difficult.

I asked him if that included his creative work. That smile again—and he said yes. This disturbed him very much. One of the reasons he had come to New York was to break things up. He had no success working in Paris in recent weeks. He worked very well in Marrakech for a few days, but Marrakech relaxed him too much in its fairy-tale world, and then he could not work, didn't want to work at all.

So he was in New York where he would rise early in the morning and write, unable to get used to the strange bed and the traffic sounds which reached up to his high room and roared all night long. He was finishing the lyrics for a children's opera, and it was coming so hard. The words were not easily supporting his ideas, and the ideas sometimes seemed impervious to the words. And New York was no better for him than Paris or Marrakech.

So we ordered matzoh-ball soup.

When the waiter put the bowls down our secret was out.

"Hey, you're Jack Brel, ain't you?"

I rolled my head upward toward the waiter who had, from his point of view, asked a very ordinary question that needed no reply, since he was scribbling our omelette order on his green pad.

"How do you know he's Brel?"

"The show. I seen the show. That's a good show, you know that?"

"But how do you know him?"

"The picture on the wall. You know, like there's a beach, and Jack is leaning out like."

"That's right."

The waiter hustled off as if the most ordinary thing had happened. It was a tiny moment, of course, but it delighted me, for we had made Brel known somewhat. Recognition by a Stage Delicatessen waiter is not to be scoffed at.

That night we went to the Village Gate to see our show. I did not want to watch from the side; I wanted to sit with Jacques; I wanted to be in it with him. I was sure of the night ahead. It was going to be pure joy—a celebration.

It was, too. Elly Stone and Mort Shuman performed brilliantly. Mort had flown in from London just to be on stage for Jacques.

Jacques Brel Is Alive and Well and Living in Paris engulfed Jacques Brel at the Village Gate. He laughed. He applauded. He forgot that I couldn't follow rapid French and he talked at me constantly. Several times he slapped my back.

At the end we both got to our feet and led the standing ovation. Jim Clark hit Brel from the control booth with a spotlight that he had rigged two years earlier for precisely this moment.

"Ladies and gentlemen: Jacques Brel!" Jim announced over the PA system. The applause lasted a very long time. I think Jacques was pleased with our little bit of hoke. We were anyway.

After the audience had left, we had a private celebration for Jacques in D'Lugoff's cellar. He collared me during the evening and he said to me, first trying for it in English and then switching to slow French: "You have really done it. You have separated me from the work. The songs have a life of their own." Then he laughed, "I really enjoyed them."

I needed photos of Jacques, Elly, and Mort, and I made that one imposition on him. The next afternoon we went down to Riverside Drive Park in the rain, and Marge Jackson Baum took the photos. It was a strange and beautiful afternoon. The four of us played at having our pictures taken, and had wonderful talks during it all.

Jacques was the one most aware of Marge at work, and occasionally he would break into a graceful lope ending with a high leap.

That night Jacques went to our show again. He told me that his pleasure in watching it was the same as the night before and he was content, *très content.*

Later we went to dinner—Elly, Mort, Jacques, and I.

Elly, who had been more tense about meeting Jacques than she had ever been about meeting anyone before, was now his great friend, just as Mort had long been, and as I had only recently become. Elly and Jacques had invented an improvisation, regarding precisely what I could not figure out. All I know is that it always ended with one of them saying, or whispering, or shouting: "La Rhumba!"

At the table Jacques toasted Elly and told us she was the finest lady performer he had ever seen. He also asked if she would play in a film he hoped to make. He would write one or two songs for her. The fact that Elly's eyes filled with tears does not matter much—good or bad, Jacques or no. She cries a lot.

The one thing we did not do at dinner was break into song. We might have done so except that Jacques was talking about flying, about the feelings of flight, about the beauty of the ocean, of air, about clouds, about men who live in clouds, about how space bends around us.

It all sounded like songs to me.

The next day was for me, Mort, and Jacques. We used it to talk about business—past business and future business. We did it all very seriously, until we realized how serious we were, and then we immediately stopped. Mort said, "Let the lawyers do it." We agreed.

The day after was get-away day for Jacques. It was also Mort's birthday. He was thirty-one. No party this time. Just Mort saying, "I'm thirty-one, you know. *Thirty-one!*"

Jacques and I looked at him, understanding the stunned look splayed over the big face that seemed so hairless in spite of his mustache and mutton chops. We took Mort to a bar and sadly celebrated the passing of Shuman's time.

Then Mort remembered he had to go.

We had a final drink and we split.

Mort Shuman (left) and Eric Blau (right) "taking ten" during rehearsals for *Jacques Brel*. Photo: Drake Studios.

Jacques in 1956.

Jacques in concert—1963. Photo: André Lemaire.

Elly Stone and Mort—very formal. Photo: Al Drake.

The original cast:
Alice Whitfield (kneeling),
Shawn Elliott (standing),
Elly, and Mort.
Photo: Bob Cato.

Mort—during "Funeral Tango." Photo: Marge Baum.

Elly—at the start of "Madeleine."
Photo: Marge Baum.

Elly—during "No, Love, You're Not Alone." Photo: Marge Baum.

Mort—while making the original cast recording at CBS.

Our mighty little cast—recording.

It takes more than an original cast—no matter how brilliant it may be—to continue a show successfully. As a matter of cold fact the better the originals the more difficult it is for the replacements. Thus, they had to be quite brilliant themselves. And they were. How very much they were.

NORMAN ATKINS

JOHN C. ATTLE

GEORGE BALL

JACK BLACKTON

J. T. CROMWELL

ROBERT GUILLAUME

JOE MASIELL

STAN PORTER

VAL PRINGLE

WAYNE SHERWOOD

HOWARD ROSS

JOE SILVER

MARGERY COHEN

CHEVI COLTON

SALLY COOKE

FLEURY DANTONAKIS

ELINOR ELLSWORTH

AILEEN FITZPATRICK

JOY FRANZ

RITA GARDNER

AMELIA HAAS

JUDY LANDER   DENISE LE BRUN   ARLENE MEADOWS

TERI RALSTON   BETTY RHODES   HENRIETTA VALOR

Wolf Knittel, me, Jacques, and Mort in what we call the dressing room at The Village Gate. Photo: Mort Shuman.

Jacques and Moni Yakim. Photo: Mort Shuman.

Jacques clowning—with Ivan Black in the doorway.
Photo: Mort Shuman.

Jacques seeing *Jacques Brel* for the first time. Photo: Mort Shuman.

Jacques on his feet at the end of the show—and me about six inches off the ground! Photo: Mort Shuman.

Here is all of 3W Productions, Inc. plus Jacques and Elly. (3W stands
for *Wehr, Wes, Wos* or Who Knows What?) (Left to right) Elly,
Norman Eisner, Stanley Swerdlow, me, Jacques, and Henry L. Hoffman. Photo: Mort Shuman.

Jacques and Mort at The Village Gate party. Photo: Mort Shuman.

Elly and Jacques at the same party. Photo: Mort Shuman.

Jacques. Photo: Mort Shuman.

A rainy day on Riverside Drive—we talked a lot. Photo: Marge Baum.

Jacques seized with irrepressible high spirits. Photo: Marge Baum.

THE SONGS / LES CHANSONS

MARATHON [1]

Join us now, we're on a marathon
We're always dancing when the music plays
Join us now, we're on a marathon
Dancing, dancing through the nights and days

We must dance because the Twenties roar
The Twenties roar because there's bathtub gin
Vo-de-o-do and the road to sin
The road to whoopee and a whole lot more

Charles A. Lindbergh, tons of confetti
Dempsey–Tunney, Sacco and Vanzetti
Black, black Monday and the market drops
But we keep on dancing, dancing, we can't stop
Marathon, marathon,
Mara, mara, marathon
Join us now, we're on a marathon
We're always dancing when the music plays
Join us now, we're on a marathon
Dancing, dancing through the nights and days

We must dance because the Thirties scream
The Thirties scream because the Horsemen ride
Orphan Annie lives, Daddy Warbucks dies
Breadlines, shanty towns, Frankenstein's bride

Adolf Hitler and the Siegfried follies
Joseph Stalin and a bag full of jollies
Call your broker and buy marzipan
While we keep on dancing, dancing on and on
Marathon, marathon

Mara, mara, marathon
Marathon, marathon
Mara, mara, marathon
Join us now, we're on a marathon
We're always dancing when the music plays
Join us now, we're on a marathon
Dancing, dancing through the nights and days

We must dance because the Forties burn
The Forties burn because the trumpets blare
The Yanks are coming, coming over there
Auschwitz, Edelweiss, Drang und Sturm

Manhattan Project, Robert Oppenheim
God makes mushrooms just as God makes time
Peace is sweet, man, like a lollipop
So we keep on dancing, dancing, we won't stop
Marathon, marathon
Mara, mara, marathon
Marathon, marathon
Mara, mara, marathon
Join us now, we're on a marathon
We're always dancing when the music plays
Join us now, we're on a marathon
Dancing, dancing through the nights and days

We must dance because the Fifties zing
The Fifties zing because the Sixties swing
And the Seventies flash and the Eighties bang
And the Nineties whimper and the century hangs
Robots working in the cotton fields
Vacations on Venus just a tourist deal
Fornication on tape, instant happiness
So we keep on dancing, dancing, we can't rest
Marathon, marathon
Mara, mara, marathon
Marathon, marathon
Mara, mara, marathon!

LES FLAMANDES [2]

Les Flamandes dansent sans rien dire
Sans rien dire aux Dimanches sonnants
Les Flamandes dansent sans rien dire
Les Flamandes ça n'est pas causant
Si elles dansent c'est parce qu'elles ont vingt ans
Et qu'à vingt ans il faut se fiancer
Se fiancer pour pouvoir se marier
Et se marier pour avoir des enfants
C'est ce que leur ont dit leurs parents
Le bedeau et même Son Eminence
L'Archiprêtre qui prêche au couvent
Et c'est pour ça et c'est pour ça qu'elles dansent
Les Flamandes
Les Flamandes
Les Fla
Les Fla
Les Flamandes

Les Flamandes dansent sans frémir
Sans frémir aux Dimanches sonnants
Les Flamandes dansent sans frémir
Les Flamandes ça n'est pas frémissant
Si elles dansent c'est parce qu'elles ont trente ans
Et qu'à trente ans il est bon de montrer
Que tout va bien que poussent les enfants
Et le houblon et le blé dans le pré
Elles font la fierté de leurs parents
Du bedeau et de son Eminence
L'Archiprêtre qui prêche au couvent
Et c'est pour ça et c'est pour ça qu'elles dansent
Les Flamandes
Les Flamandes
Les Fla
Les Fla
Les Flamandes

Les Flamandes dansent sans sourire
Sans sourire aux Dimanches sonnants
Les Flamandes dansent sans sourire
Les Flamandes ça n'est pas souriant
Si elles dansent c'est qu'elles ont septante ans
Qu'à septante ans il est bon de montrer
Que tout va bien que poussent les petits enfants
Et le houblon et le blé dans le pré
Toutes vêtues de noir comme leurs parents
Comme le bedeau et comme Son Eminence
L'Archiprêtre qui radote au couvent
Elles héritent et c'est pour ça qu'elles dansent
Les Flamandes
Les Flamandes
Les Fla
Les Fla
Les Flamandes

Les Flamandes dansent sans mollir
Sans mollir aux Dimanches sonnants
Les Flamandes dansent sans mollir
Les Flamandes ça n'est pas mollissant
Si elles dansent c'est parce qu'elles ont cent ans
Et qu'à cent ans il est bon de montrer
Que tout va bien qu'on a toujours bon pied
Et bon houblon et bon blé dans le pré
Elles s'en vont retrouver leurs parents
Le bedeau et même Son Eminence
L'Archiprêtre qui repose au couvent
Et c'est pour ça qu'une dernière fois elles dansent
Les Flamandes
Les Flamandes
Les Fla
Les Fla
Les Flamandes

ALONE [3]

We find love, you and I
It's a new game to play
Then we tell our first lie
And see love go away
And we find . . . we're alone

We rush on, you and I
We don't need love at all
We need thrills, we need speed
Then we stumble and fall
And we find . . . we're alone

We're loyal, you and I
To flowers that are dead
We forget how to cry
We save photos instead
And we find . . . we're alone

We hear guns, you and I
We ask what is that
Then we open the *Times*
We're informed where it's at
And we find . . . we're alone

We're moral, you and I
We stand for what's right
We slaughter all evil
By dawn's early light
And we find . . . we're alone

We're lucky, you and I
We're alive and secure
But in the bank and the church

We can never feel sure
And we find . . . we're alone

We've made it, you and I
We have glory and fame
Yet we never know why
We feel so ashamed
And we find . . . we're alone

We have power, you and I
But what good is that now
We would build a new world
If we only knew how
And we find . . . we're alone

We are old, you and I
We beg warmth from the sun
In the dreams that we dream
We ask what have we done
And we find . . . we're alone

SEUL [4]

On est deux mon amour
Et l'amour chante et rit
Mais à la mort du jour
Dans les draps de l'ennui
On se retrouve seul

On est dix à défendre
Les vivants par des morts
Mais cloués par leurs cendres
Au poteau du remords
On se retrouve seul

On est cent qui dansons
Au bal des bons copains
Mais au dernier lampion
Mais au premier chagrin
On se retrouve seul

On est mille contre mille
A se croire les plus forts
Mais à l'heure imbécile
Où ça fait deux mille morts
On se retrouve seul

On est million à rire
Du million qui est en face
Mais deux millions de rires
N'empêchent que dans la glace
On se retrouve seul

On est mille à s'asseoir
Au sommet de la fortune
Mais dans la peur de voir
Tout fondre sous la lune
On se retrouve seul

On est cent que la gloire
Invite sans raison
Mais quand meurt le hasard
Quand finit la chanson
On se retrouve seul

On est dix à coucher
Dans le lit de la puissance
Mais devant ces armées
Qui s'enterrent en silence
On se retrouve seul

On est deux à vieillir
Contre le temps qui cogne
Mais lorsqu'on voit venir

En riant la charogne
On se retrouve seul

MADELEINE [5]

I'm waiting for Madeleine
In front of the picture show
Every night at half past ten
Madeleine, she loves that so
I'm waiting for Madeleine
We'll go down and eat at Joe's
The french fries are from who knows when
But Madeleine she loves them so
Madeleine's my Christmas tree
She's America to me
I know that she's too good for me
  (That's what her mother always says)
I'm waiting for Madeleine
We'll go to the picture show
I'll tell her that I love her then
Madeleine, she loves that so
  She is much more than pretty
  She is all that you know
  She is my whole life to me
  I love my Madeleine so, so
I'm waiting for Madeleine
But I'm getting soaking wet
I've been soaked since half past ten

Madeleine is not here yet
I'm waiting for Madeleine
Joe is closed by now I'll bet
No french fries from who knows when
Madeleine is not here yet
Madeleine's my shining sea
She's America to me
I know that she's too good for me
   (That's what her father always says)
I'm waiting for Madeleine
I've still got the picture show
I'll tell her that I love her then
Madeleine, she'll love that so
   She is much more than pretty
   She is all that you know
   She is my whole life to me
   I love my Madeleine so, so
I waited for Madeleine
I only have myself to blame
I went and caught a cold again
Madeleine, she never came
I waited for Madeleine
All I did was call her name
A thousand times since half past ten
Madeleine, she never came
Madeleine's my " 'Tis of Thee"
She's America to me
It's true that she's too good for me
   (That's what her brother alway says)
I waited for Madeleine
It's always been the same
Waiting here since who knows when
Madeleine, she never came
   She is much more than pretty
   She is all that you know
   She is my whole life to me
   I love my Madeleine so, so
I'm gonna wait for Madeleine
In front of the picture show

Tomorrow night at half past ten
Madeleine, she'll love that so
I'm gonna wait for Madeleine
We'll go down and eat at Joe's
The french fries are from who knows when
But Madeleine, she loves them so
Madeleine's my Christmas tree
She's America to me
So what if she's too good for me
    (Her mother?)
I'm gonna wait for Madeleine
We'll go to the picture show
I'll tell her that I love her then
Madeleine, she'll love that so—oooh!

MADELEINE [6]

Ce soir j'attends Madeleine
J'ai apporté du lilas
J'en apporte toutes les semaines
Madeleine elle aime bien ça
Ce soir j'attends Madeleine
On prendra le tram trente-trois
Pour manger des frites chez Eugène
Madeleine elle aime tant ça
Madeleine c'est mon Noël
C'est mon Amérique à moi
Même qu'elle est trop bien pour moi
Comme dit son cousin Joël
Ce soir j'attends Madeleine
On ira au cinéma
Je lui dirai des « je t'aime »
Madeleine elle aime tant ça

Elle est tellement jolie
Elle est tellement tout ça
Elle est toute ma vie
Madeleine que j'attends là

Ce soir j'attends Madeleine
Mais il pleut sur mes lilas
Il pleut comme toutes les semaines
Et Madeleine n'arrive pas
Ce soir j'attends Madeleine
C'est trop tard pour le tram trente-trois
Trop tard pour les frites d'Eugène
Et Madeleine n'arrive pas
Madeleine c'est mon horizon
C'est mon Amérique à moi
Même qu'elle est trop bien pour moi
Comme dit son cousin Gaston
Mais ce soir j'attends Madeleine
Il me reste le cinéma
Je lui dirai des « je t'aime »
Madeleine elle aime tant ça

Elle est tellement jolie
Elle est tellement tout ça
Elle est toute ma vie
Madeleine qui n'arrive pas

Ce soir j'attendais Madeleine
Mais j'ai jeté mes lilas
Je les ai jetés comme toutes les semaines
Madeleine ne viendra pas
Ce soir j'attendais Madeleine
C'est fichu pour le cinéma
Je reste avec mes « je t'aime »
Madeleine ne viendra pas
Madeleine c'est mon espoir
C'est mon Amérique à moi
Sûr qu'elle est trop bien pour moi
Comme dit son cousin Gaspard

Ce soir j'attendais Madeleine
Tiens le dernier tram s'en va
On doit fermer chez Eugène
Madeleine ne viendra pas

Elle est tellement jolie
Elle est tellement tout ça
Elle est toute ma vie
Madeleine qui ne viendra pas

Demain j'attendrai Madeleine
Je rapporterai du lilas
J'en rapporterai toute la semaine
Madeleine elle aimera ça
Demain j'attendrai Madeleine
On prendra le tram trente-trois
Pour manger des frites chez Eugène
Madeleine elle aimera ça
Madeleine c'est mon espoir
C'est mon Amérique à moi
Tant pis si elle est trop bien pour moi
Comme dit son cousin Gaspard
Demain j'attendrai Madeleine
On ira au cinéma
Je lui dirai des « je t'aime »
Madeleine elle aimera ça

I LOVED [7]

I loved all games and fairy tales
As strangely odd as that may seem
I loved firelight and witches' tales
You see, you were there in my dreams

I lived in a tower, cloud-top high
To stop your love from passing by
For this I simply had to do
You see, I was waiting for you

I loved the rocks, the ocean breeze
And the hissing of the foam
The wild, wild kiss of the roaring seas
Now, you had brought me home

You leaped buildings in single bounds
Although I well may ask you how
You bayed the moon just like a hound
I knew I adored you now

You laced the night with raging storms
You threw lightning 'cross the skies
You kissed my mouth with promises
You burned me with your lies

You loved me like a poet loves
My nights were made of stars and fears
Thinking that you would go away
And leave me with only my tears

I loved the towns where we made love
And the hotels where we played games
You thought I'd never live it down
Yet you see, I've forgotten your name

J'AIMAIS [8]

J'aimais les fées et les princesses
Qu'on me disait n'exister pas
J'aimais le feu et la tendresse
Tu vois je vous rêvais déjà

J'aimais les tours hautes et larges
Pour voir au large venir l'amour
J'aimais les tours de cœur de garde
Tu vois je vous guettais déjà

J'aimais le col ondoyant des vagues
Les saules nobles languissant vers moi
J'aimais la ligne tournante des algues
Tu vois je vous savais déjà

J'aimais courir jusqu'à tomber
J'aimais la nuit jusqu'au matin
Je n'aimais rien non j'ai adoré
Tu vois je vous aimais déjà

J'aimais l'été pour ses orages
Et pour la foudre sur le toit
J'aimais l'éclair sur ton visage
Tu vois je vous brûlais déjà

J'aimais le pluie noyant l'espace
Au long des brumes du pays plat
J'aimais la brume que le vent chasse
Tu vois je vous pleurais déjà

J'aimais la vigne et le houblon
Les villes du Nord les laides de nuit
Les fleuves profonds m'appelant au lit
Tu vois je vous oubliais déjà

MATHILDE [9]

Momma, do you see what I see
On your knees and pray for me
Mathilde's come back to me
Charley, don't want another beer
Tonight I'm gonna drink my tears
Mathilde's come back to me
Go ask the maid if she heard what I said
Tell her to change the sheets on the bed
Mathilde's come back to me
Fellas, don't leave me tonight
Tonight I'm going back to fight
Wretched Mathilde's in sight

My heart, my heart, stop beating so
Just make as if you didn't know
That Mathilde's come back to me
My heart, I don't want you to say
She's lovelier than when she went away
Mathilde, who's come back to me
My heart, stop being overjoyed
Remember you were once destroyed
By Mathilde, who's come back to me
Fellas, please don't go away
Tell me that I mustn't stay
Mathilde's coming back today

My hands, you'll start to shake again
When you remember all the pain
Mathilde's come back to me
You'll want to beat her black and blue
But don't do it, I beg of you
Mathilde's come back to me
My hands, remember all the years
Remember when you caught my tears

Mathilde's come back to me
My hands, you'll want to touch her now
But please try and be strong somehow
Mathilde's here, she's coming now, now

Momma, can you hear me yell
Your baby boy's gone back to hell
Mathilde's come back to me
Charley, champagne right away
I know you've been saving it for the holiday
But Mathilde's come back to me
Go ask the maid if she heard what I said
Tell her to put the best sheets on the bed
Mathilde's come back to me
My friends, don't count on me no more
I've gone and crashed through heaven's door
My sweet Mathilde's here
Once more, once more

MATHILDE [10]

Ma mère voici le temps venu
D'aller prier pour mon salut
Mathilde est revenue
Bougnat tu peux garder ton vin
Ce soir je boirai mon chagrin
Mathilde est revenue
Toi la servante toi la Maria
Vaudrait peut-être mieux changer nos draps
Mathilde est revenue
Mes amis ne me laissez pas
Ce soir je repars au combat
Maudite Mathilde puisque te v'là

Mon cœur mon cœur ne t'emballe pas
Fais comme si tu ne savais pas
Que la Mathilde est revenue
Mon cœur arrête de répéter
Qu'elle est plus belle qu'avant l'été
La Mathilde qui est revenue
Mon cœur arrête de bringuebaler
Souviens-toi qu'elle t'a déchiré
La Mathilde qui est revenue
Mes amis ne me laissez pas
Dites-moi dites-moi qu'il ne faut pas
Maudite Mathilde puisque te v'là

Et vous mes mains restez tranquilles
C'est un chien qui nous revient de la ville
Mathilde est revenue
Et vous mes mains ne frappez pas
Tout ça ne vous regarde pas
Mathilde est revenue
Et vous mes mains ne tremblez plus
Souvenez-vous quand je vous pleurais dessus
Mathilde est revenue
Vous mes mains ne vous ouvrez pas
Vous mes bras ne vous tendez pas
Sacrée Mathilde puisque te v'là

Ma mère arrête tes prières
Ton Jacques retourne en enfer
Mathilde m'est revenue
Bougnat apporte-nous du vin
Celui des noces et des festins
Mathilde m'est revenue
Toi la servante toi la Maria
Va tendre mon grand lit de draps
Mathilde m'est revenue
Amis ne comptez plus sur moi
Je crache au ciel encore une fois
Ma belle Mathilde puisque te v'là te v'là

BACHELOR'S DANCE [11]

The girl that I will marry
Will have a heart so wise
That in the hollow of her eyes
My heart will want to tarry

The girl who will be mine
Will have skin so soft and tender
And when it comes December
Her skin will be my wine

And me, I'll love her so
And she, she will love me
And our hearts burning slow
For at least a century

Through the window of life
We will go as girl and boy
To become man and wife
To become one with joy

No, it isn't you
The girl that I will marry
No, it isn't you
The girl who'll marry me

The girl that I will love
Will have a house of grace
All painted white, and there my soul
Will find its hiding place

The girl that I will love
Will do her vigil keeping

And late at night she'll tell me of
The children that are sleeping

And me, I'll love her so
And she, she will love me
We'll make a present of our love
To us and destiny

And we will take the sun
To dress our love in gold
For soon our youth is gone
For soon we must grow old

No, it isn't you
The girl that I will love
No, it isn't you
The girl that will love me

The girl that I will marry
Will age with happiness
For she will have a fireplace
And all my tenderness

The girl that I will marry
Will age without a fear
And like the wine grow mellower
With every passing year

And me, I'll love her so
And she, she will love me
And we will write a song
For all the joys that used to be

And when we leave this earth
Our eyes still filled with love
We'll send a flower down to hell
And up to heaven above

Ah, won't she come to me

The girl that I will marry
Who will she be
The girl who'll marry me

LA BOURRÉE DU CÉLIBATAIRE [12]

La fille que j'aimera
Aura le cœur si sage
Qu'au creux de son visage
Mon cœur s'arrêtera
La fille que j'aimera
Je lui veux la peau tendre
Pour qu'aux nuits de décembre
S'y réchauffent mes doigts
Et moi je l'aimerons
Et elle m'aimera
Et nos cœurs brûleront
Du même feu de joie
Entrerons en chantant
Dans les murs de la vie
En offrant nos vingt ans
Pour qu'elle nous soit jolie
Non ce n'est pas toi
La fille que j'aimerons
Non ce n'est pas toi
La fille que j'aimera

La fille que j'aimera
Aura sa maison basse
Blanche et simple à la fois
Comme un état de grâce
La fille que j'aimera
Aura des soirs de veille

Où elle me parlera
Des enfants qui sommeillent
Et moi je l'aimerons
Et elle m'aimera
Et nous nous offrirons
Tout l'amour que l'on a
Pavoiserons tous deux
Notre vie de soleil
Avant que d'être vieux
Avant que d'être vieille
Non ce n'est pas toi
La fille que j'aimerons
Non ce n'est pas toi
La fille que j'aimera

La fille que j'aimera
Vieillira sans tristesse
Entre son feu de bois
Et ma grande tendresse
La fille que j'aimera
Sera comme bon vin
Qui se bonifiera
Un peu chaque matin
Et moi je l'aimerons
Et elle m'aimera
Et ferons des chansons
De nos anciennes joies
Et quitterons la terre
Les yeux pleins l'un de l'autre
Pour fleurir tout l'enfer
Du bonheur qui est nôtre
Ah qu'elle vienne à moi
La fille que j'aimerons
Ah qu'elle vienne à moi
La fille que j'aimera

TIMID FRIEDA [13]

Timid Frieda
Will they greet her
On the street where
Young strangers travel
On magic carpets
Floating lightly
In beaded caravans
Who can know if
They will free her
On the street where
She comes to join them
There she goes
With her valises
Held so tightly in her hands

Timid Frieda
Will life seize her
On the street where
The new dreams gather
Like fearless robins
Joined together
In high-flying bands
She feels taller
Troubles smaller
On the street where
She's lost in wonder
There she goes
With her valises
Held so tightly in her hands

Timid Frieda
Won't return now
To the home where
They do not need her

But always feed her
Little lessons
And platitudes from cans
She is free now
She will be now
On the street where
The beat's electric
There she goes
With her valises
Held so tightly in her hands

Timid Frieda
Who will lead her
On the street where
The cops all perish
For they can't break her
And she can take her
Brave new fuck you stand
Yet she's frightened
Her senses heightened
On the street where
The darkness brightens
There she goes
With her valises
Held so tightly in her hands

Timid Frieda
If you see her
On the street where
The future gathers
Just let her be her
Let her play in
The broken times of sand
There she goes now
Down the sidewalk
On the street where
The world is bursting
There she goes
With her valises
Held so tightly in her hands

LES TIMIDES [14]

Les timides
Ça s'tortille
Ça s'entortille
Ça sautille
Ça s'met en vrille
Ça s'recroqueville
Ça rêve d'être un lapin
Peu importe
D'où ils sortent
Mais feuilles mortes
Quand l'vent les porte
Devant nos portes
On dirait qu'ils portent
Une valise dans chaque main

Les timides
Suivent l'ombre
L'ombre sombre
De leur ombre
Seule la pénombre
Sait le nombre
De leurs pudeurs de Levantin
Ils se plissent
Ils palissent
Ils jaunissent
Ils rosissent
Ils rougissent
S'écrevissent
Une valise dans chaque main

Mais les timides
Un soir d'audace
Devant leur glace
Rêvant d'espace
Mettent leur cuirasse

Et alors place
Allons Paris tiens toi bien
Et vive la gare
St. Lazare
Mais on s'égare
On s'effare
On s'désempare
Et on repart
Une valise dans chaque main

Les timides
Quand ils chavirent
Pour une Elvire
Ont des soupirs
Ont des désirs
Qu'ils désirent dire
Mais ils n'osent pas bien
Et leurs maitresses
Plus prêtresses
En ivresse
Qu'en tendresse
Un soir les laisse
Du bout des fesses
Une valise dans chaque main.

Les timides
Alors vieillissent
Alors finissent
Se rapetissent
Et quand ils glissent
Dans les Abysses
Je veux dire quand ils meurent
N'osent rien dire
Rien maudire
N'osent frémir
N'osent sourire
Juste un soupir
Et ils meurent
Un' valise sur le coeur

MY DEATH [15]

My death waits like an old roué
So confident I'll go his way
Whistle for him and the passing time
My death waits like a Bible truth
At the funeral of my youth
Weep loud for that and the passing time
My death waits like a witch at night
As surely as our love is bright
Let's laugh for us and the passing time

But whatever is behind the door
There is nothing much to do
Angel or devil, I don't care
For in front of that door there is you

My death waits like a beggar blind
Who sees the world with an unlit mind
Throw him a dime for the passing time
My death waits to allow my friends
A few good times before it ends
Let's drink to that and the passing time
My death waits in your arms, your thighs
Your cool fingers will close my eyes
Let's not talk about the passing time

But whatever is behind the door
There is nothing much to do
Angel or devil, I don't care
For in front of that door there is you

My death waits among falling leaves
In magicians' mysterious sleeves
Rabbits, doves and the passing time
My death waits there among the flowers

Where that blackest shadow cowers
Let's pick lilacs for the passing time
My death waits in a double bed
Sails of oblivion at my head
Pull up the sheets against the passing time

But whatever is behind the door
There is nothing much to do
Angel or devil, I don't care
For in front of that door there is you

LA MORT [16]

La mort m'attend comme une vieille fille
Au rendez-vous de la faucille
Pour mieux cueillir le temps qui passe
La mort m'attend comme une princesse
A l'enterrement de ma jeunesse
Pour mieux pleurer le temps qui passe
La mort m'attend comme Carabosse
A l'incendie de nos noces
Pour mieux rire du temps qui passe

Mais qu'y a-t-il derrière la porte
Et qui m'attend déjà
Ange ou démon qu'importe
Au devant de la porte il y a toi

La mort attend sous l'oreiller
Que j'oublie de me réveiller
Pour mieux glacer le temps qui passe
La mort attend que mes amis
Me viennent voir en pleine nuit

Pour mieux se dire que le temps passe
La mort m'attend dans tes mains claires
Qui devront fermer mes paupières
Pour mieux quitter le temps qui passe

Mais qu'y a-t-il derrière la porte
Et qui m'attend déjà
Ange ou démon qu'importe
Au devant de la porte il y a toi

La mort m'attend aux dernières feuilles
De l'arbre qui fera mon cercueil
Pour mieux clouer le temps qui passe
La mort m'attend dans les lilas
Qu'un fossoyeur lancera sur moi
Pour mieux fleurir le temps qui passe
La mort m'attend dans un grand lit
Tendu aux toiles de l'oubli
Pour mieux fermer le temps qui passe

Mais qu'y a-t-il derrière la porte
Et qui m'attend déjà
Ange ou démon qu'importe
Au devant de la porte il y a toi

GIRLS AND DOGS [17]

The girls
Are as fast as a game
Are as bright as a flame
And you're always to blame

The girls
Are as pink as the light
Are as dark as the night
And they're always right

The girls
Are as cold as the sphinx
Always dreaming of minks
They drive you to drink

The girls
Are as soft as a sigh
That whispers good-bye
And leaves you to cry

But the dogs
Well, they're only dogs
Just wagging their tails
As they watch it end

Oh, the dogs
Well they're only dogs
And maybe that's why
They're man's best friend

The girls
Can make you feel cold
Can make you feel old
An antique to be sold

The girls
They play with your heart
They tear you apart
You're never too smart

The girls
They throw you from towers
They'll whip you with flowers
It depends on the hours

:: **127**

The girls
Will treat you like trash
Or let you be brash
It depends on your cash

But the dogs
Don't depend on a thing
They just lick your face
When they see it end

Oh, the dogs
Don't depend on a thing
And maybe that's why
They're man's best friend

The girls
They're not what they seem
They all have a scheme
They call it a dream

The girls
Are as hot as they please
And you're down on your knees
With the greatest of ease

The girls
Say you're on the right track
Then they take it all back
Tie it up in a sack

The girls
They will give it of course
But they give with such force
That it gives you remorse

But the dogs
They give nothing at all
They just lift a leg
As they watch it end

Oh, the dogs
They give nothing at all
And that's the reason why
They're man's best friend

And yet it's because of the girls
When they've knocked us about
And our tears want to shout
That we kick the dogs out

LES FILLES ET LES CHIENS [18]

Les filles
C'est beau comme un jeu
C'est beau comme un feu
C'est beaucoup trop peu
Les filles
C'est beau comme un fruit
C'est beau comme la nuit
C'est beaucoup d'ennuis
Les filles
C'est beau comme un renard
C'est beau comme un retard
C'est beaucoup trop tard
Les filles
C'est beau tant que ça peut
C'est beau comme l'adieu
Et c'est beaucoup mieux
Mais les chiens
C'est beau comme des chiens
Et ça reste là
A nous voir pleurer
Les chiens

Ça ne nous dit rien
C'est peut-être pour ça
Qu'on croit les aimer

Les filles
Ça vous pend au nez
Ça vous prend au thé
Ça vous prend les dés
Les filles
Ça vous pend au cou
Ça vous pend au clou
Ça dépend de vous
Les filles
Ça vous pend au cœur
Ça se pend aux fleurs
Ça dépend des heures
Les filles
Ça dépend de tout
Ça dépend surtout
Ça dépend des sous
Mais les chiens
Ça ne dépend de rien
Et ça reste là
A nous voir pleurer
Les chiens
Ça ne nous dit rien
C'est peut-être pour ça
Qu'on croit les aimer

Les filles
Ça joue au cerceau
Ça joue du cerveau
Ça se joue tango
Les filles
Ça joue l'amadou
Ça joue contre joue
Ça se joue de vous
Les filles
Ça joue à jouer

Ça joue à aimer
Ça joue pour gagner
Les filles
Qu'elles jouent les petites femmes
Qu'elles jouent les grandes dames
Ça se joue en drames
Mais les chiens
Ça ne joue à rien
Parce que ça ne sait pas
Comment faut tricher
Les chiens
Ça ne joue à rien
C'est peut-être pour ça
Qu'on croit les aimer

Les filles
Ça donne à rêver
Ça donne à penser
Ça vous donne congé
Les filles
Ça se donne pourtant
Ça se donne un temps
Ça donnant donnant
Les filles
Ça donne de l'amour
A chacun son tour
Ça donne sur la cour
Les filles
Ça vous donne son corps
Ça se donne si fort
Que ça donne des remords
Mais les chiens
Ça ne vous donne rien
Parce que ça ne sait pas
Faire semblant de donner
Les chiens
Ça ne vous donne rien
C'est peut-être pour ça
Qu'on doit les aimer

Et c'est pourtant pour les filles
Qu'au moindre matin
Qu'au moindre chagrin
On renie ses chiens

JACKIE [19]

And if one day I should become
A singer with a Spanish bum
Who sings for women of great virtue
I'd sing to them with a guitar
I borrowed from a coffee bar
Well, what you don't know doesn't hurt you
My name would be Antonio
And all my bridges I would burn
And if I gave them some they'd know
I expect something in return
I'd have to get drunk every night
To talk about virility
With some old grandmother who might
Be decked out like a Christmas tree
And tho' pink elephants I'd see
I'd sing the song they sang to me
About the time they called me Jackie

If I could be for only an hour
If I could be for an hour every day
If I could be for just one little hour
Cute, cute, cute in a stupid-ass way

And if I joined the social whirl
Became procurer of young girls
Then I would have my own bordellos
My record would be number one
And I'd sell records by the ton
All sung by many other fellows
My name would then be handsome Jack
And I'd sell boats of opium
Whiskey that came from Twickenham
Authentic queers and phony virgins
I'd have a bank on every finger
A finger in every country
And every country ruled by me
I still know where I'd want to be
Locked up inside my opium den
Surrounded by some Chinamen
I'd sing the song that I sang then
About the time they called me Jackie

If I could be for only an hour
If I could be for an hour every day
If I could be for just one little hour
Cute, cute, cute in a stupid-ass way

Now tell me wouldn't it be nice
That if one day in Paradise
I sang for all the ladies up there
And they would sing along with me
We'd be so happy there to be
'Cause down below is really nowhere
My name would then be Jupiter
And I would know where I was going
And then I would become all knowing
With my beard so long and flowing
If I became deaf dumb and blind
Because I pitied all mankind
And broke my heart to make things right
I know that every single night
When my angelic work was through

The angels and the devil too
Would sing my childhood song to me
About the time they called me Jackie

If I could be for only an hour
If I could be for an hour every day
If I could be for just one little hour
Cute, cute, cute in a stupid-ass way

JACKY [20]

Même si un jour à Knocke le Zoute
Je deviens comm' je le redoute
Chanteur pour femmes finissantes
Même si leur chant "mi corazon"
Avec la voix bandonéante
D'un argentin de Carcassonne

Même si on m'appell' Antonio
Que je brûle mes derniers feux
En échang' de quelques cadeaux
Madam' je fais ce que je peux

Même si j'me saoûle a l'hydromel'
Pour mieux parler d'virilité
À des mémères decorées
Commes des arbres de Noël

Chaque nuit dans ma saoullographie
Pour un public d'éléphants roses
Je chant'rai la chanson morose
Celle du temps où j'm'applait Jacky

Être un'heure un'heure seulement
Être un'heure un'heure quelquefois
Être un'heure rien qu'un heur' durant
Beau beau et con à la fois

Même si un jour à Macao
Je d'viens gouverneur de tripot
Cerclé de femmes languissantes
Même si lassé d'être chanteur
J'y sois dev'nu maître chanteur
Et qu'ce soit les autres qui chantent

Même si on m'appell' le beau Serge
Que je vende des bateaux d'opium
Du whisky de Clermont Ferrand
De vrais pédés de fausses vierges

Que j'ai une banque à chaque doigt
Et un doigt dans chaque pays
Que chaque pays soit à moi
Je sais quand même que chaque nuit

Tout seul au fond de ma fumerie
Pour un public de vieux chinois
Je chant'rai ma chanson à moi
Celle du temps où j'm'applait Jacky

Être un'heure un'heure seulement
Être un'heure un'heure quelquefois
Être un'heure rien qu'un heur' durant
Beau beau et con à la fois

Même si un jour à Paradis
Je devienne comm' j'en s'rais surpris
Chanteur pour femmes à ailes blanches
Même si leur chant' alleluia

En regrettant le temps d'en bas
Où c'est pas tous les jours dimanche

Même si on m'appell' Dieu le Père
Celui qui est dans l'annuaire
Entre Dieu l'fit et Dieu vos garde
Même si je m'laisse pousser la barbe

Même si toujours trop bonne pomm'
Je m'crève le cœur et l'pur esprit
À vouloir consoler les hommes
Je sais quand même que chaque nuit

J'entendrai dans mon paradis
Les Anges les Saints et Lucifer
Me chanter ma chanson d'naguère
Celle du temps où j'm'applait Jacky

Être un'heure un'heure seulement
Être un'heure un'heure quelquefois
Être un'heure rien qu'un heur' durant
Beau beau et con à la fois

THE STATUE [21]

I'd like to grab that son of Mary
The one who wrote on my statue
"He has lived all of his life
Between honor and virtue"
Me, who screwed all of my friends
From dirty lie to dirty lie

Me, who screwed all of my friends
From New Year's Day to New Year's Day
In the purest name of love
How I cheated every mistress
In the purest name of love
How I lied with each caress
That son of Mary I'd like to have him here
And all you damned kids . . . get out of here

I'd like to grab that son of Lent
The one who had the nerve to boast
"God calls back the ones he loves
And he was the one God loved the most"
Me, who only prayed to God
When my teeth were killing me
Me, who only prayed to God
Except when I was scared of Satan
Me, who even prayed to Satan
Everytime I was in love
Me, who even prayed to Satan
Whenever I was scared of God
That son of Lent I'd like to have him here
And all you damned kids . . . get out of here

I'd like to grab that son-of-a-bitch
The one who wrote on my statue
"He died like a hero
He was a soldier brave and true"
Me, who went off to the war
Because I was so damn bored
Me, who went off to the war
To make it with the German broads
Me, who got killed in the war
Making it with the German broads
Me, who died during the war
Because I couldn't help it
That son-of-a-bitch, I'd like to have him here
And all you damned kids . . . Please
Please get out of here

LA STATUE [22]

J'aimerais tenir l'enfant de Marie
Qui a fait graver sous ma statue
« Il a vécu toute sa vie
Entre l'honneur et la vertu »
Moi qui ai trompé mes amis
De faux serment en faux serment
Moi qui ai trompé mes amis
Du jour de l'An au jour de l'An
Moi qui ai trompé mes maîtresses
De sentiment en sentiment
Moi qui ai trompé mes maîtresses
Du printemps jusques au printemps
Cet enfant de Marie je l'aimerais là
Et j'aimerais que les enfants ne me regardent pas

J'aimerais tenir l'enfant de carême
Qui a fait graver sous ma statue
«Les Dieux rappellent ceux qu'ils aiment,
Et c'était lui qu'ils aimaient le plus »
Moi qui n'ai jamais prié Dieu
Que lorsque j'avais mal aux dents
Moi qui n'ai jamais prié Dieu
Que quand j'ai eu peur de Satan
Moi qui n'ai prié Satan
Que lorsque j'étais amoureux
Moi qui n'ai prié Satan
Que quand j'ai eu peur du Bon Dieu
Cet enfant de carême je l'aimerais là
Et j'aimerais que les enfants ne me regardent pas

J'aimerais tenir l'enfant de salaud
Qui a fait graver sous ma statue
« Il est mort comme un héros
Il est mort comme on ne meurt plus »

Moi qui suis parti faire la guerre
Parce que je m'ennuyais tellement
Moi qui suis parti faire la guerre
Pour voir si les femmes des Allemands
Moi qui suis mort à la guerre
Parce que les femmes des Allemands
Moi qui suis mort à la guerre
De n'avoir pu faire autrement
Cet enfant de salaud je l'aimerais là
Et j'aimerais que mes enfants ne me regardent pas

THE DESPERATE ONES [23]

They hold each other's hand
They walk without a sound
Down forgotten streets
Their shadows kiss the ground
Their footsteps sing a song
That's ended before it's begun
They walk without a sound
The desperate ones

Just like the tiptoe moth
They dance before the flame
They've burned their hearts so much
That death is just a name
And if love calls again
So foolishly they run
They run without a sound
The desperate ones

I know the road they're on
I've walked their crooked mile
A hundred times or more
I drank their cup of bile
They watch their dreams go down
Behind the setting sun
They walk without a sound
The desperate ones

And underneath the bridge
The waters sweet and deep
There is the journey's end
The land of endless sleep
They cry to us for help
We think it's all in fun
They cry without a sound
The desperate ones

Let he who threw the stone at them
Stand up and take a bow
He knows the verb to love
But he'll never know how
On the bridge of nevermore
They disappear one by one
Disappear without a sound
The desperate ones

LES DÉSESPÉRÉS [24]

Se tiennent par la main
Et marchent en silence
Dans ces villes éteintes
Que le crachin balance

Ne sonnent que leurs pas
Pas à pas fredonnés

Ils marchent en silence
Les désespérés

Ils ont brûlé leurs ailes
Ils ont perdu leurs branches
Tellement naufragés
Que la mort paraît blanche
Ils reviennent d'amour
Ils se sont reveillés

Ils marchent en silence
Les désespérés

Et je sais leur chemin
Pour l'avoir cheminé
Déjà plus de cent fois
Cent fois plus qu'à moitié
Moins vieux ou plus meurtris
Ils vont le terminer

Ils marchent en silence
Les désespérés

Et en dessous du pont
L'eau est douce et profonde
Voici la bonne hôtesse
Voici la fin du monde
Ils pleurent leurs prénoms
Comm'de jeunes mariés

Et fondent en silence
Les désespérés

Que se lève celui
Qui leur lance la pierre
Il ne sait de l'amour
Que le verbe s'aimer
Sur le pont n'est plus rien
Qu'une brume légère

Ça s'oublie en silence
Ceux qui ont espéré

SONS OF [25]

Sons of the thief, sons of the saint
Who is the child with no complaint
Sons of the great or sons unknown
All were children like your own
The same sweet smiles, the same sad tears
The cries at night, the nightmare fears
Sons of the great or sons unknown
All were children like your own. . . .

So long ago: long, long, ago. . . .

But sons of tycoons or sons of the farms
All of the children ran from your arms
Through fields of gold, through fields of ruin
All of the children vanished too soon
In tow'ring waves, in walls of flesh
Among dying birds trembling with death

Sons of tycoons or sons of the farms
All of the children ran from your arms. . . .

So long ago: long, long, ago. . . .

But sons of your sons or sons passing by
Children we lost in lullabies
Sons of true love or sons of regret
All of the sons you cannot forget
Some built the roads, some wrote the poems
Some went to war, some never came home
Sons of your sons or sons passing by
Children we lost in lullabies. . . .

So long ago: long, long, ago. . . .

But, sons of the thief, sons of the saint
Who is the child with no complaint
Sons of the great or sons unknown
All were children like your own
The same sweet smiles, the same sad tears
The cries at night, the nightmare fears
Sons of the great or sons unknown
All were children like your own. . . .

Like your own, like your own, like your own

FILS DE [26]

Fils de bourgeois ou fils d'apôtre
Tous les enfants sont comme les vôtres
Fils de César ou fils de rien
Tous les enfants sont comme le tien

Le même sourire, les mêmes larmes
Les mêmes alarmes, les mêmes soupirs
Fils de César ou fils de rien
Tous les enfants sont comme le tien

Ce n'est qu'après, longtemps apres. . . .

Mais fils de Sultan, fils de fakir
Tous les enfants ont un empire
Sous voute d'or, sous toit de chaume
Tous les enfants ont un royaume
Un coin de vague, une fleur qui tremble
Un oiseau mort qui leur ressemble
Fils de Sultan, fils de fakir
Tous les enfants ont un empire

Ce n'est qu'après, longtemps apres. . . .

Mais fils de ton fils ou fils d'étranger
Tous les enfants sont des sorciers
Fils de l'amour, fils d'amourette
Tous les enfants sont des poètes
Ils sont bergers, ils sont rois mages
'S ont des nuages pour mieux voler
Fils de ton fils ou fils d'étranger
Tous les enfants sont des sorciers

Ce n'est qu'après, longtemps apres. . . .

Mais fils de bourgeois ou fils d'apôtre
Tous les enfants sont comme les vôtres
Fils de César ou fils de rien
Tous les enfants sont comme le tien
Les mêmes sourires, les mêmes larmes
Les mêmes alarmes, les mêmes soupirs
Fils de César ou fils de rien
Tous les enfants sont comme le tien. . . .

In the port of Amsterdam
There's a sailor who sings
Of the dreams that he brings
From the wide open sea
In the port of Amsterdam
There's a sailor who sleeps
While the riverbank weeps
With the old willow tree
In the port of Amsterdam
There's a sailor who dies
Full of beer, full of cries
In a drunken down fight
And in the port of Amsterdam
There's a sailor who's born
On a muggy hot morn
By the dawn's early light

In the port of Amsterdam
Where the sailors all meet
There's a sailor who eats
Only fishheads and tails
He will show you his teeth
That have rotted too soon
That can swallow the moon
That can haul up the sails
And he yells to the cook
With his arms open wide
Bring me more fish
Put it down by my side
Then he wants so to belch
But he's too full to try
So he gets up and laughs
And he zips up his fly

In the port of Amsterdam
You can see sailors dance
Paunches bursting their pants
Grinding woman to paunch
They've forgotten the tune
That their whiskey voice croaks
Splitting the night with the
Roar of their jokes
And they turn and they dance
And they laugh and they lust
Till the rancid sound of
The accordion bursts
Then out to the night
With their pride in their pants
With the slut that they tow
Underneath the streetlamps

In the port of Amsterdam
There's a sailor who drinks
And he drinks and he drinks
And he drinks once again
He drinks to the health
Of the whores of Amsterdam
Who have promised their love
To one thousand other men
They've bargained their bodies
And their virtue long gone
For a few dirty coins
And when he can't go on
He plants his nose in the sky
And he wipes it up above
And he pisses like I cry
For an unfaithful love

In the port of Amsterdam
In the port of Amsterdam

AMSTERDAM [28]

Dans le port d'Amsterdam
Il y a des marins qui chantent
Les rêves qui les hantent
Au large d'Amsterdam
Dans le port d'Amsterdam
Il y a des marins qui dorment
Comme des oriflammes
Le long des berges mornes
Dans le port d'Amsterdam
Il y a des marins qui meurent
Pleins de bière et de drames
Aux premières lueurs
Dans le port d'Amsterdam
Il y a des marins qui naissent
Dans la chaleur épaisse
Des langueurs océanes

Dans le port d'Amsterdam
Il y a des marins qui mangent
Sur des nappes trop blanches
Des poissons ruisselants
Ils vous montrent des dents
A croquer la fortune
A décroisser la lune
A bouffer des haubans
Et ça sent la morue
Jusque dans le cœur des frites
Que leurs grosses mains invitent
A revenir en plus
Puis se lèvent en riant
Dans un bruit de tempête
Referment leur braguette
Et sortent en rotant

Dans le port d'Amsterdam
Il y a des marins qui dansent
En se frottant la panse
Sur la panse des femmes
Et ils tournent et ils dansent
Comme des soleils crachés
Dans le son déchiré
D'un accordéon rance
Ils se tordent le cou
Pour mieux s'entendre rire
Jusqu'à ce que tout à coup
L'accordéon expire
Alors d'un geste grave
Alors le regard fier
Ils ramènent leur batave
Jusqu'en pleine lumière

Dans le port d'Amsterdam
Il y a des marins qui boivent
Et qui boivent et reboivent
Et qui reboivent encore
Ils boivent à la santé
Des putains d'Amsterdam
De Hambourg ou d'ailleurs
Enfin ils boivent aux dames
Qui leur donnent leur joli corps
Qui leur donnent leur vertu
Pour une pièce en or
Et quand ils ont bien bu
Se plantent le nez au ciel
Se mouchent dans les étoiles
Et ils pissent comme je pleure
Sur les femmes infidèles

THE BULLS [29]

On Sundays the bulls get so bored
When they are asked to show off for us
There is the sun, the sand, and the arena
There are the bulls ready to bleed for us
It's the time when grocery clerks become Don Juan
It's the time when all ugly girls
Turn into swans, aaahh.

Who can say of what he's found
That bull who turns and paws the ground
And suddenly he sees himself all nude, aaahh.
Who can say of what he dreams
That bull who hears the silent screams
From the open mouths of multitudes.

Olé!

On Sundays the bulls get so bored
When they are asked to suffer for us
There are the picadors and the mob's revenge
There are the toreros, and the mob kneels for us
It's the time when grocery clerks become García Lorca
And the girls put roses in the teeth like Carmen.

On Sundays the bulls get so bored
When they are asked to drop dead for us
The sword will plunge down and the mob will drool
The blood will pour down and turn the sand to mud.

Olé, olé!

The moment of triumph when grocery clerks become Nero
The moment of triumph when the girls scream and shout
The name of their hero, aaahh.

And when finally they fell
Did not the bulls dream of some hell
Where men and worn-out matadors still burn, aaahh.
Or perhaps with their last breaths
· Would not they pardon us their deaths
Knowing what we did at
Carthage—olé!—Waterloo—olé—Verdun—olé!
Stalingrad—olé!—Iwo Jima—olé!—Hiroshima—olé!—Saigon!

LES TOROS [30]

Les toros s'ennuient le dimanche
Quand il s'agit de courir pour nous
Un peu de sable du soleil et des planches
Un peu de sang pour faire un peu de boue
C'est l'heure où les épiciers se prennent pour Don Juan
C'est l'heure où les Anglaises se prennent pour Montherlant
Ah!
Qui nous dira à quoi ça pense
Un toro qui tourne et danse
Et s'aperçoit soudain qu'il est tout nu
Ah!
Qui nous dira à quoi ça rêve
Un toro dont l'œil se lève
Et qui découvre les cornes des cocus

Les toros s'ennuient le dimanche
Quand il s'agit de souffrir pour nous
Voici les picadors et la foule se venge
Voici les toreros et la foule est à genoux
C'est l'heure où les épiciers se prennent pour García Lorca
C'est l'heure où les Anglaises se prennent pour la Carmencita

Les toros s'ennuient le dimanche
Quand il s'agit de mourir pour nous
Mais l'épée va plonger et la foule se penche
Mais l'épée a plongé et la foule est debout
C'est l'instant de triomphe où les épiciers se prennent pour Néron
C'est l'instant de triomphe où les Anglaises se prennent pour
    Wellington
Ah!

Est-ce qu'en tombant à terre
Les toros rêvent d'un enfer
Où brûleraient hommes et toreros défunts
Ah!
Ou bien à l'heure du trépas
Ne nous pardonneraient-ils pas
En pensant à Carthage Waterloo et Verdun
Verdun

THE OLD FOLKS [31]

The old folks don't talk much
And they talk so slowly when they do
They are rich, they are poor, their illusions are gone
They share one heart for two
Their homes all smell of thyme, of old photographs
And an old-fashioned song
Though you may live in town you live so far away
When you've lived too long
And have they laughed too much, do their dry voices crack

Talking of times gone by
And have they cried too much, a tear or two
Still always seems to cloud the eye
They tremble as they watch the old silver clock
When day is through
It tick-tocks oh so slow, it says, "Yes," it says, "No"
It says, "I'll wait for you."

The old folks dream no more
The books have gone to sleep, the piano's out of tune
The little cat is dead and no more do they sing
On a Sunday afternoon
The old folks move no more, their world's become too small
Their bodies feel like lead
They might look out the window or else sit in a chair
Or else they stay in bed
And if they still go out, arm in arm, arm in arm
In the morning's chill
It's to have a good cry, to say their last good-bye
To one who's older still
And then they go home to the old silver clock
When day is through
It tick-tocks oh so slow, it says, "Yes," it says, "No"
It says, "I'll wait for you."

The old folks never die
They just put down their heads and go to sleep one day
They hold each other's hand like children in the dark
But one will get lost anyway
And the other will remain just sitting in that room
Which makes no sound
It doesn't matter now, the song has died away
And echoes all around
You'll see them when they walk through the sun-filled park
Where children run and play
It hurts too much to smile, it hurts too much but life goes on
For still another day
As they try to escape the old silver clock
When day is through

It tick-tocks oh so slow, it says, "Yes," it says, "No"
It says, "I'll wait for you."

The old, old silver clock that's hanging on the wall
That waits for us
All.

LES VIEUX [32]

Les vieux ne parlent plus ou alors seulement parfois du bout des
    yeux
Même riches ils sont pauvres ils n'ont plus d'illusions et n'ont qu'un
    cœur pour deux
Chez eux ça sent le thym le propre la lavande et le verbe d'antan
Que l'on vive à Paris on vit tous en province quand on vit trop
    longtemps
Est-ce d'avoir trop ri que leur voix se lézarde quand ils parlent
    d'hier
Et d'avoir trop pleuré que des larmes encore leur perlent aux
    paupières
Et s'ils tremblent un peu est-ce de voir vieillir la pendule d'argent
Qui ronronne au salon qui dit oui qui dit non qui dit je vous
    attends

Les vieux ne rêvent plus leurs livres s'ensommeillent leurs pianos
    sont fermés
Le petit chat est mort le muscat du dimanche ne les fait plus
    chanter
Les vieux ne bougent plus leurs gestes ont trop de rides leur monde
    est trop petit
Du lit à la fenêtre puis du lit au fauteuil et puis du lit au lit
Et s'ils sortent encore bras dessus bras dessous tout habillés de
    raide

C'est pour suivre au soleil l'enterrement d'un plus vieux l'enterre-
    ment d'une plus laide
Et le temps d'un sanglot oublier toute une heure la pendule d'argent
Qui ronronne au salon qui dit oui qui dit non et puis qui les attend

Les vieux ne meurent pas ils s'endorment un jour et dorment trop
    longtemps
Ils se tiennent la main ils ont peur de se perdre et se perdent
    pourtant
Et l'autre reste là le meilleur ou le pire le doux ou le sévère

Cela n'importe pas celui des deux qui reste se retrouve en enfer
Vous le verrez peut-être vous la verrez parfois en pluie et en chagrin
Traverser le présent en s'excusant déjà de n'être pas plus loin
Et fuir devant vous une dernière fois la pendule d'argent
Qui ronronne au salon qui dit oui qui dit non qui leur dit je
    t'attends
Qui ronronne au salon qui dit oui qui dit non et puis qui nous
    attend

MARIEKE [33]

Ay, Marieke, Marieke
The Flanders sun burns the sky
Since you are gone
Ay, Marieke, Marieke
In Flanders field the poppies die
Since you are gone

Zonder liefde, warme liefde
Waait de wind de stomme wind
Zonder liefde, warme liefde
Weent de zee de grijze zee
Zonder liefde, warme liefde
Lijdt het licht het donk're licht
En schuurt het zand over mijn land
Mijn platte land mijn Vlanderland

Ay, Marieke, Marieke
The stars look down, so soon, so soon
The day is done
Ay, Marieke, Marieke
The Flanders moon won't light your way
The day is gone

Zonder liefde, warme liefde
Waait de wind c'est fini
Zonder liefde, warme liefde
Weent de zee déjà fini
Zonder liefde, warme liefde
Lijdt het licht tout est fini
En schuurt het zand over mijn land
Mijn platte land mijn Vlanderland

Ay, Marieke, Marieke
The bells have rung, the echoes sound
The day is gone
Ay, Marieke, Marieke
In Flanders field the echoes sound
The day is gone

Zonder liefde, warme liefde
Lacht duivel de zwarte duivel
Zonder liefde, warme liefde
Brandt mijn hart mijn oude hart
Zonder liefde, warme liefde
Sterft de zomer de droeve zomer
En schuurt het zand over mijn land
Mijn platte land mijn Vlanderland

Ay, Marieke, Marieke
Come back again, come back again
The day is gone
Ay, Marieke, Marieke
Your love alone, your love alone
The day is gone

Ay, Marieke, Marieke
Come back again, come back again
The day is gone
Ay, Marieke, Marieke
Your love alone, your love alone
The day is gone, the day is gone, the day is gone

MARIEKE [34]

Ay Marieke Marieke je t'aimais tant
Entre les tours de Bruges et Gand
Ay Marieke Marieke il y a longtemps
Entre les tours de Bruges et Gand

Zonder liefde warme liefde
Waait de wind de stomme wind
Zonder liefde warme liefde
Weent de zee de grijze zee
Zonder liefde warme liefde
Lijdt het licht het donk're licht
En schuurt het zand over mijn land
Mijn platte land mijn Vlaanderland

Ay Marieke Marieke le ciel flamand
Couleur des tours de Bruges et Gand

[34] Copyright © 1961, 1968 by Editions Philippe Pares, Paris. Used by Permission.

Ay Marieke Marieke le ciel flamand
Pleure avec moi de Bruges à Gand

Zonder liefde warme liefde
Waait de wind c'est fini
Zonder liefde warme liefde
Weent de zee déjà fini
Zonder liefde warme liefde
Lijdt het licht tout est fini
En schuurt het zand over mijn land
Mijn platte land mijn Vlaanderland

Ay Marieke Marieke le ciel flamand
Pesait-il trop de Bruges à Gand
Ay Marieke Marieke sur tes vingt ans
Que j'aimais tant de Bruges à Gand

Zonder liefde warme liefde
Lacht de duivel de zwarte duivel
Zonder liefde warme liefde
Brandt mijn hart mijn oude hart
Zonder liefde warme liefde
Sterft de zomer de droeve zomer
En schuurt het zand over mijn land
Mijn platte land mijn Vlaanderland

Ay Marieke Marieke revienne le temps
Revienne le temps de Bruges et Gand
Ay Marieke Marieke revienne le temps
Où tu m'aimais de Bruges à Gand

Ay Marieke Marieke le soir souvent
Entre les tours de Bruges et Gand
Ay Marieke Marieke tous les étangs
M'ouvrent leurs bras de Bruges à Gand
De Bruges à Gand de Bruges à Gand

It was the time when Brussels could sing
It was the time of the silent movies
It was the time when Brussels was king
It was the time when Brussels brustled
Pick out a hat so dashing and gay
Go take a walk, it's a beautiful day
Put on your spats and your high-buttoned shoes
Get on the tram, get the gossip and news

Not a time for crying
How the heart was flying
There was my grandfather
There was my grandmother
He was a young soldier
She was so much bolder
He had no brains, neither did she
How bright could I turn out to be?

Oh, it was the time when Brussels could sing
It was the time of the silent movies
It was the time when Brussels was king
It was the time when Brussels brustled
Pick out a dress so dashing and gay
Go take a walk, it's a beautiful day
Put on your spats and your high-buttoned shoes
Get on the tram, get the gossip and news

Not a time for crying
How the heart was flying
There was my grandfather
There was my grandmother
He knew how to do it

And she let him do it
They lived in sin—deliciously
Now they pray for my virginity

Oh, it was the time when Brussels could sing
It was the time of the silent movies
It was the time when Brussels was king
It was the time when Brussels brustled
Sing out a song so dashing and gay
Walk hand-in-hand, it's a beautiful day
Hop on the tram with your high-buttoned shoes
Dance on the tram to the gossip and news

Not a time for crying
How the heart was flying
There was my grandfather
There was my grandmother
Ten million guns got loaded
World War I exploded
It was such fun—oh, what a game
They saved the world but I bring it shame

It was the time when Brussels could sing
It was the time of the silent movies
It was the time when Brussels was king
It was the time when
It was the time when
It was the time when Brussels could sing
It was the time of the silent movies
It was the time when Brussels was king
It was the time when Bruuuuuuuhhhhhhhhhhh!

BRUXELLES [36]

C'était au temps où Bruxelles rêvait
C'était au temps du cinéma muet
C'était au temps où Bruxelles chantait
C'était au temps où Bruxelles bruxellait

Place de Broukère on voyait des vitrines
Avec des hommes des femmes en crinoline
Place de Broukère on voyait l'omnibus
Avec des femmes des messieurs en gibus
Et sur l'impériale
Le cœur dans les étoiles
Il y avait mon grand-père
Il y avait ma grand-mère
Il était militaire
Elle était fonctionnaire
Il pensait pas elle pensait rien
Et on voudrait que je sois malin

C'était au temps où Bruxelles chantait
C'était au temps du cinéma muet
C'était au temps où Bruxelles rêvait
C'etait au temps où Bruxelles bruxellait

Sur les pavés de la place Sainte-Catherine
Dansaient les hommes les femmes en crinoline
Sur les pavés dansaient les omnibus
Avec des femmes des messieurs en gibus
Et sur l'impériale
Le cœur dans les étoiles
Il y avait mon grand-père
Il y avait ma grand-mère
Il avait su y faire
Elle l'avait laissé faire
Ils l'avaient donc fait tous les deux
Et on voudrait que je sois sérieux

C'était au temps où Bruxelles rêvait
C'était au temps du cinéma muet
C'était au temps où Bruxelles dansait
C'était au temps où Bruxelles bruxellait

Sous les lampions de la place Sainte-Justine
Chantaient les hommes les femmes en crinoline
Sous les lampions dansaient les omnibus
Avec des femmes des messieurs en gibus
Et sur l'impériale
Le cœur dans les étoiles
Il y avait mon grand-père
Il y avait ma grand-mère
Il attendait la guerre
Elle attendait mon père
Ils étaient gais comme le canal
Et on voudrait que j'aie le moral

C'était au temps où Bruxelles rêvait
C'était au temps du cinéma muet
C'était au temps où Bruxelles chantait
C'était au temps où Bruxelles bruxellait

FANETTE [37]

We were two friends in love, Fanette and I
The empty beach was warm and sleepy in July
If the sea recalls, the waves would surely say
I sang so many songs for Fanette each day

She was, she was as beautiful as rainbows in the sky
She was so beautiful and not at all am I
She was, she was there on the sand as gold as she was brown
And when I held her hand I held the world around
I was, I was so crazy then to think that it could be
I thought that I was hers, I believed she was for me
But we, we never learn until it's too late

We were two friends in love, Fanette and I
The empty beach was warm deceitful in July
If the sea recalls, the waves would surely say
I stopped singing my songs for Fanette that day

I saw, I saw them arm-in-arm enfolded by the sea
They looked so much in love they never looked at me
They saw, they saw me and they laughed, they stood and watched
    me cry
And sang their little song, I cursed the summer sky
You see, I'd like to tell you how
They swam so well that day
They swam so far away
You'll never see them now
Oh, no, no, no, no, no—no, we never learn
But let's talk of something else

We were never two friends, Fanette and I
The empty streets are cold and crying in July
But when the waves are still I still can hear it yet
I hear a little song
I hear
Fanette

LA FANETTE [38]

Nous étions deux amis et Fanette m'aimait
La plage était déserte et dormait sous juillet
Si elles s'en souviennent les vagues vous diront
Combien pour la Fanette j'ai chanté de chansons

>Faut dire
>Faut dire qu'elle était belle
>Comme une perle d'eau
>Faut dire qu'elle était belle
>Et je ne suis pas beau
>Faut dire
>Faut dire qu'elle était brune
>Tant la dune était blonde
>Et tenant l'autre et l'une
>Moi je tenais le monde
>Faut dire
>Faut dire que j'étais fou
>De croire à tout cela
>Je le croyais à nous
>Je la croyais à moi
>Faut dire
>Qu'on ne nous apprend pas
>A se méfier de tout

Nous étions deux amis et Fanette m'aimait
La plage était déserte et mentait sous juillet
Si elles s'en souviennent les vagues vous diront
Comment pour la Fanette s'arrêta la chanson

>Faut dire
>Faut dire qu'en sortant
>D'une vague mourante
>Je les vis s'en allant

Comme amant et amante
Faut dire
Faut dire qu'ils ont ri
Quand ils m'ont vu pleurer
Faut dire qu'ils ont chanté
Quand je les ai maudits
Faut dire
Que c'est bien ce jour-là
Qu'ils ont nagé si loin
Qu'ils ont nagé si bien
Qu'on ne les revit pas
Faut dire
Qu'on ne nous apprend pas
Mais parlons d'autre chose

Nous étions deux amis et Fanette l'aimait
La place est déserte et pleure sous juillet
Et le soir quelquefois
Quand les vagues s'arrêtent
J'entends comme une voix
J'entends . . . c'est la Fanette

FUNERAL TANGO [39]

Ah, I can see them now
Clutching a handkerchief
And blowing me a kiss
Discreetly asking how

How come he died so young
Or was he very old
Is the body warm
Is it already cold

All doors are open wide
They poke around inside
My desk, my drawers, my trunk
There's nothing left to hide

Some love letters are there
And an old photograph
They've laid my poor soul bare
And all they do is laugh
Ha, ha, ha, ha, ha—ha, ha, ha!

Ah, I can see them all
So formal and so stiff
Like a sergeant-at-arms
At the policemen's ball

And everybody's pushing
To be the first in line
Their hearts upon their sleeves
Like a ten-cent valentine

The old women are there
Too old to give a damn
They even brought the kids
Who don't know who I am

They're thinking about the price
Of my funeral bouquet
What they're thinking isn't nice
'Cause now they'll have to pay
Ha, ha, ha, ha, ha—ha, ha, ha!

Ah, I see all of you
All of my phoney friends

Who can't wait till it ends
Who can't wait till it's through

Oh, I see all of you
You've been laughing all these years
And now all that you have left
Are a few crocodile tears

Ah, you don't even know
That you're entering your hell
As you leave my cemetery
And you think you're doing well

With that one who's at your side
You're as proud as you can be
Ah, she's going to make you cry
But not the way you cried for me
Ha, ha, ha, ha, ha—ha, ha, ha!

Ah, I can see me now
So cold and so alone
As the flowers slowly die
In my field of little bones

Ah, I can see me now
I can see me at the end
Of this voyage that I'm on
Without a love, without a friend

Now, all this that I see
Is not what I deserve
They really have a nerve
To say these things to me

No, girls, just bread and water
All your money you must save
Or there'll be nothing left for us
When you're dead and in your grave
Ha, ha, ha, ha, ha—ha, ha, ha!

LE TANGO FUNÈBRE [40]

Ah je les vois déjà
Me couvrant de baisers
Et s'arrachant mes mains
Et demandant tout bas
Est-ce que la mort s'en vient
Est-ce que la mort s'en va
Est-ce qu'il est encore chaud
Est-ce qu'il est déjà froid
Ils ouvrent mes armoires
Ils tâtent mes faïences
Ils fouillent mes tiroirs
Se régalant d'avance
De mes lettres d'amour
Enrubannées par deux
Qu'ils liront près du feu
En riant aux éclats
Ah Ah Ah Ah Ah Ah

Ah je les vois déjà
Compassés et frileux
Suivant comme des artistes
Mon costume de bois
Ils se poussent du cœur
Pour être le plus triste
Ils se poussent du bras
Pour être le premier
Z'ont amené des vieilles
Qui ne me connaissaient plus
Z'ont amené des enfants
Qui ne me connaissaient pas
Pensent aux prix des fleurs
Et trouvent indécent
De ne pas mourir au printemps

Quand on aime le lilas
Ah Ah Ah Ah Ah Ah

Ah je les vois déjà
Tous mes chers faux amis
Souriant sous le poids
Du devoir accompli
Ah je te vois déjà
Trop triste trop à l'aise
Protégeant sous le drap
Tes larmes lyonnaises
Tu ne sais même pas
Sortant de mon cimetière
Que tu entres en ton enfer
Quand s'accroche à ton bras
Le bras de ton quelconque
Le bras de ton dernier
Qui te fera pleurer
Bien autrement que moi
Ah Ah Ah Ah Ah Ah

Ah je me vois déjà
M'installant à jamais
Bien triste bien au froid
Dans mon champ d'osselets
Ah je me vois déjà
Je me vois tout au bout
De ce voyage-là
D'où l'on revient de tout
Je vois déjà tout ça
Et on a le brave culot
D'oser me demander
De ne plus boire que de l'eau
De ne plus trousser les filles
De mettre de l'argent de côté
D'aimer le filet de maquereau
Et de crier vive le roi
Ah Ah Ah Ah Ah Ah

THE MIDDLE CLASS [41]

Your heart feels so right
Your eyes swim in the beer
Where the barroom lights are hung
With your friend Jojo
With your friend Pierre
You drink a toast to being young
Jojo thinks he's Voltaire
And Pierre, Casanova
And me who proudly did not care
Me, I was a lover
And at midnight we watched the
Lawyers pass
Coming out of hotels which had real class

We showed them our good manners
And we showed them our ass
And, oh, how we sang

The middle class are just like pigs
The older they get, the dumber they get
The middle class are just like pigs
The fatter they get, the less they regret

Your heart feels so right
Your eyes swim in the beer
Where the barroom lights are hung
With your friend Jojo
With your friend Pierre
Holding on to being young
Voltaire danced like a vicar
Casanova, he was too stout
And me who proudly did not care
Me, I drank till I passed out
And at midnight

We watched the salesmen pass
Coming out of hotels which had real class

We showed them our good manners
And we showed them our ass
And, oh, how we sang

The middle class are just like pigs
The older they get, the dumber they get
The middle class are just like pigs
The fatter they get, the less they regret

But your heart slows down
Your eyes do not flash
The hotel bartender sings our praise

Jojo's no clown
Pierre pays in cash
Among the bookkeepers we pass our days
Jojo now speaks of Voltaire
Casanova's just a book on the shelf
And, me, I proudly do not care
Me, I talk only of myself
And everybody knows
That we've got real class
There is not a night that we can pass
Those lousy kids
Who always show us their ass
And, oh, how they sing

The middle class are just like pigs
The older they get, the dumber they get
The middle class are just like pigs
The fatter they get, the less they regret

LES BOURGEOIS [42]

Le cœur bien au chaud
Les yeux dans la bière
Chez la grosse Adrienne de Montalant
Avec l'ami Jojo
Et avec l'ami Pierre
On allait boire nos vingt ans
Jojo se prenait pour Voltaire
Et Pierre pour Casanova
Et moi, qui étais le plus fier
Moi, je me prenais pour moi
Et quand vers minuit passaient les notaires
Qui sortaient de l'Hôtel « Des Trois Faisans »
On leur montrait notr' cul et nos bonn's manières
En leur chantant

Les bourgeois c'est comm' les cochons
Plus ça devient vieux, plus ça devient bête
Les bourgeois c'est comm' les cochons
Plus ça devient, vieux plus ça devient . . .

Le cœur bien au chaud
Les yeux dans la bière
Chez la grosse Adrienne de Montalant
Avec l'ami Jojo
Et avec l'ami Pierre
On allait brûler nos vingt ans
Voltair' dansait comme un vicaire
Et Casanova n'osait pas
Et moi, qui étais le plus fier
Moi, je me prenais pour moi
Et quand vers minuit passaient les notaires
Qui sortaient de l'Hôtel « Des Trois Faisans »
On leur montrait notr' cul et nos bonn's manières
En leur chantant

Les bourgeois c'est comm' les cochons
Plus ça devient vieux, plus ça devient bête
Les bourgeois c'est comm' les cochons
Plus ça devient vieux, plus ça devient . . .

Le cœur au repos
Les yeux bien sur terre
Au bar de l'Hôtel «Des Trois Faisans »
Avec Maître Jojo
Et avec Maître Pierre
Entre notaires on pass' le temps
Jojo parle de Voltaire
Et Pierre de Casanova
Et moi, qui suis resté le plus fier
Moi, je parle encore de moi
Et c'est en sortant Monsieur l' Commissaire
Que tous les soirs de chez la Montalant
De jeunes « peigne-culs » nous montrent leur derrière
En leur chantant

Les bourgeois c'est comm' les cochons
Plus ça devient vieux, plus ça devient bête
Les bourgeois c'est comm' les cochons
Plus ça devient vieux, plus ça devient . . .

NO, LOVE, YOU'RE NOT ALONE [43]

No, love, you're not alone
It's all right if you cry
If things don't turn out right
All we can do is try
We'll see a show tonight
There's something we can buy
No, love, you're not alone
Don't let it get you down
It's just another day
And everything's turned brown
You've walked your bloody mile
I'll hold you for a while
No, love, you're not alone
I swear the sun will rise
I promise you you'll laugh
Here, love, dry your eyes
Come on.

Come, we've got each other now
That's got to be enough
Pretend you're really tough, love
Come on, love, come on
We've got each other now
And if that's not enough
Remember being young
The days all strung with bells
We caught the sea in shells
We conquered wishing wells
And songs of carousels, love
And if you still feel sad
Remember making love, it really wasn't bad
When that was all we had
The paradise in bed, remember that instead
Instead of all these sorrows

So rest here in my arms, love
For we still hold tomorrow

No, love, you're not alone
No matter how you feel
When shadows cut like knives
And none of this seems real
We wish away our lives
Yet somehow we survive
No, love, you're not alone
Your wounds one day will heal
Perhaps you feel too much
And maybe that's the crime
Perhaps you pray too much
And there isn't any shrine
No, love, you're not alone
I swear the earth will stay
White doves will soon fly down
I promise you your day
Come on.

Come. We'll sing old melodies
We'll sit with birds in trees
And sing for whom it pleases
Love, come on
We'll dance across the moon
Turn midnight into noon
Pour perfume on the breezes
Where nothing ever grows
Where no one ever goes
In lands of storms and snows
We'll plant one burning rose, love
And, if you still feel sad
I'll seize the passing years
I'll squeeze out all the tears
The newsreel of our life
I'll play it in reverse
Your pain will fall away
We'll relive yesterday

And start where we began, love
We'll do it if we can, love
We'll do it if we can. . . .
Come on, love. Come on. Come on. Come on.

JEF [44]

Non Jef t'es pas tout seul
Mais arrête de pleurer
Comme ça devant tout le monde
Parce qu'une demi-vieille
Parce qu'une fausse blonde
T'a relaissé tomber
Non Jef t'es pas tout seul
Mais tu sais que tu me fais honte
A sangloter comme ça
Bêtement devant tout le monde
Parce qu'une trois quarts putain
T'a claqué dans les mains
Non Jef t'es pas tout seul
Mais tu fais honte à voir
Les gens se paient notre tête
Foutons le camp de ce trottoir
Allez viens Jef viens viens

Viens il me reste trois sous
On va aller se les boire
Chez la mère Françoise
Viens il me reste trois sous
Et si c'est pas assez
Ben il me restera l'ardoise
Puis on ira manger
Des moules et puis des frites

Des frites et puis des moules
Et du vin de Moselle
Et si t'es encore triste
On ira voir les filles
Chez la madame Andrée
Paraît qu'y en a de nouvelles
On rechantera comme avant
On sera bien tous les deux
Comme quand on était jeune
Comme quand c'était le temps
Que j'avais de l'argent

Non Jef t'es pas tout seul
Mais arrête tes grimaces
Soulève tes cent kilos
Fais bouger ta carcasse
Je sais que t'as le cœur gros
Mais faut le soulever
Non Jef t'es pas tout seul
Mais arrête de sangloter
Arrête de te répandre
Arrête de répéter
Que t'es bon à te foutre à l'eau
Que t'es bon à te pendre
Non Jef t'es pas tout seul
Mais c'est plus un trottoir
Ça devient un cinéma
Où les gens viennent te voir
Allez viens Jef viens viens

Viens il me reste ma guitare
Je l'allumerai pour toi
Et on sera espagnols
Comme quand on était mômes
Même que j'aimais pas ça
T'imiteras le rossignol
Puis on se trouvera un banc
On parlera de l'Amérique
Où c'est qu'on va aller

Quand on aura du fric
Et si t'es encore triste
Ou rien que si t'en as l'air
Je te raconterai comment
Tu deviendras Rockefeller
On sera bien tous les deux
On rechantera comme avant
Comme quand on était beaux
Comme quand c'était le temps
D'avant qu'on soit poivrots

Allez viens Jef viens viens viens
Oui oui Jef oui viens

NEXT [45]

Naked as sin, an army towel
Covering my belly
Some of us blush, somehow
Knees turning to jelly
Next, next.

I was still just a kid
There were a hundred like me
I followed a naked body
A naked body followed me
Next, next.

I was still just a kid
When my innocence was lost

In a mobile army whorehouse
Gift of the army, free of cost
Next, next.

Me, I really would have liked
A little touch of tenderness
Maybe a word, a smile
An hour of happiness
But, next, next.

Oh, it wasn't so tragic
The high heavens did not fall
But how much of that time
I hated being there at all
Next, next.

Now I always will recall
The brothel truck, the flying flags
The queer lieutenant who slapped
Our asses as if we were fags
Next, next.

I swear on the wet head
Of my first case of gonorrhea
It is his ugly voice
That I forever hear
Next, next.

That voice that stinks of whiskey
Of corpses and of mud
It is the voice of nations
It is the thick voice of blood
Next, next.

And since then each woman
I have taken to bed
Seems to laugh in my arms
To whisper through my head
Next, next.

All the naked and the dead
Should hold each other's hands
As they watch me scream at night
In a dream no one understands
Next, next.

And when I am not screaming
In a voice grown dry and hollow
I stand on endless naked lines
Of the following and the followed
Next, next.

One day I'll cut my legs off
Or burn myself alive
Anything, I'll do anything
To get out of line to survive
Not ever to be next
Not ever to be next.

AU SUIVANT [46]

Tout nu dans ma serviette qui me servait de pagne
J'avais le rouge au front et le savon à la main
      Au suivant au suivant
J'avais juste vingt ans et nous étions cent vingt
A être le suivant de celui qu'on suivait
      Au suivant au suivant
J'avais juste vingt ans et je me déniaisais
Au bordel ambulant d'une armée en campagne
      Au suivant au suivant

Moi j'aurais bien aimé un peu plus de tendresse
Ou alors un sourire ou bien avoir le temps

                Mais au suivant au suivant
Ce ne fut pas Waterloo mais ce ne fut pas Arcole
Ce fut l'heure où l'on regrette d'avoir manqué l'école
                Au suivant au suivant
Mais je jure que d'entendre cet adjudant de mes fesses
C'est des coups à vous faire des armées d'impuissants
                Au suivant au suivant

Je jure sur la tête de ma première vérole
Que cette voix depuis je l'entends toute le temps
                Au suivant au suivant
Cette voix qui sentait l'ail et le mauvais alcool
C'est la voix des nations et c'est la voix du sang
                Au suivant au suivant
Et depuis chaque femme à l'heure de succomber
Entre mes bras trop maigres semble me murmurer
                Au suivant au suivant

Tous les suivants du monde devraient se donner la main
Voilà ce que la nuit je crie dans mon délire
                Au suivant au suivant
Et quand je ne délire pas j'en arrive à me dire
Qu'il est plus humiliant d'être suivi qui suivant
                Au suivant au suivant
Un jour je me ferai cul-de-jatte ou bonne sœur ou pendu
Enfin un de ces machins où je ne serai jamais plus
                Le suivant le suivant

Carnivals and cotton candy
Carousels and calliopes
Fortune-tellers in glass cases
We will always remember these
Merry-go-rounds quickly turning
Quickly turning for you and me
And the whole world madly turning
Turning, turning 'till you can't see

We're on a carousel
A crazy carousel
And now we go around
Again we go around
And now we spin around
We're high above the ground
And down again around
And up again around
So high above the ground
We feel we've got to yell
We're on a carousel
A crazy carousel
We're on a ferris wheel
A crazy ferris wheel
A wheel within a wheel
And suddenly we feel
The stars begin to reel
And down again around
And up again around
And up again around
So high above the ground
We feel we've got to yell
We're on a carousel
A crazy carousel

Carnivals and cotton candy
Carousels and calliopes
Crazy clowns chasing brass rings
Soda pop and rock-candy trees
Merry-go-rounds quickly turning
Quickly turning for you and me
And the whole world madly turning
Turning, turning 'till you can't see

We're on a carousel
A crazy carousel
And now we go around
Again we go around
And now we spin around
We're high above the ground
And down again around
And up again around
So high above the ground
We feel we've got to yell
We're on a carousel
A crazy carousel
We're on a ferris wheel
A crazy ferris wheel
A wheel within a wheel
And suddenly we feel
The stars begin to reel
And down again around
And up again around
And up again around
So high above the ground
We feel we've got to yell
We're on a carousel
A crazy carousel
We're on a carousel
A crazy carousel
And now we go around
Again we go around
And now we spin around
We're high above the ground

And down again around
And up again around
So high above the ground
We feel we've got to yell
We're on a carousel
A crazy carousel

Carnivals and cotton candy
Carousels and calliopes
Kewpie-dolls with painted faces
Tricky shell games and missing peas
Merry-go-rounds quickly turning
Quickly turning for you and me
And the whole world madly turning
Turning, turning 'till you can't see

We're on a carousel
A crazy carousel
And now we go around
Again we go around
And now we spin around
We're high above the ground
And down again around
And up again around
So high above the ground
We feel we've got to yell
We're on a carousel
A crazy carousel
We're on a ferris wheel
A crazy ferris wheel
A wheel within a wheel
And suddenly we feel
The stars begin to reel
And down again around
And up again around
And up again around
So high above the ground
We feel we've got to yell
We're on a carousel

A crazy carousel
We're on a carousel
A crazy carousel
And now we go around
Again we go around
And now we spin around
We're high above the ground
And down again around
And up again around
So high above the ground
We feel we've got to yell
We're on a carousel
A crazy carousel
La, la, la, la—la, la, la, la
La, la, la—la, la, la, la, la—la!

LA VALSE À MILLE TEMPS [48]

Au premier temps de la valse
Toute seule tu souris déjà
Au premier temps de la valse
Je suis seul mais je t'aperçois
Et Paris qui bat la mesure
Paris qui mesure notre émoi
Et Paris qui bat la mesure
Me murmure murmure tout bas

Une valse à trois temps
Qui s'offre encore le temps
Qui s'offre encore le temps
De s'offrir des détours
Du côté de l'amour
Comme c'est charmant
Une valse à quatre temps

C'est beaucoup moins dansant
C'est beaucoup moins dansant
Mais tout aussi charmant
Qu'une valse à trois temps
Une valse à quatre temps
Une valse à vingt ans
C'est beaucoup plus troublant
C'est beaucoup plus troublant
Mais beaucoup plus charmant
Qu'une valse à trois temps
Une valse à vingt ans
Une valse à cent temps
Une valse à cent temps
Une valse ça s'entend
A chaque carrefour
Dans Paris que l'amour
Rafraîchit au printemps
Une valse à mille temps
Une valse à mille temps
Une valse a mis l' temps
De patienter vingt ans
Pour que tu aies vingt ans
Et pour que j'aie vingt ans
Une valse à mille temps
Une valse à mille temps
Une valse à mille temps
Offre seule aux amants
Trois cent trente-trois fois le temps
De bâtir un roman

Au deuxième temps de la valse
On est deux tu es dans mes bras
Au deuxième temps de la valse
Nous comptons tous les deux une deux trois
Et Paris qui bat la mesure
Paris qui mesure notre émoi
Et Paris qui bat la mesure
Nous fredonne déjà

Une valse à trois temps
Qui s'offre encore le temps
Qui s'offre encore le temps
De s'offrir des détours
Du côté de l'amour
Comme c'est charmant
Une valse à quatre temps
C'est beaucoup moins dansant
C'est beaucoup moins dansant
Mais tout aussi charmant
Qu'une valse à trois temps
Une valse à quatre temps
Une valse à vingt ans
C'est beaucoup plus troublant
C'est beaucoup plus troublant
Mais beaucoup plus charmant
Qu'une valse à trois temps
Une valse à vingt ans
Une valse à cent temps
Une valse à cent temps
Une valse ça s'entend
A chaque carrefour
Dans Paris que l'amour
Rafraîchit au printemps
Une valse à mille temps
Une valse à mille temps
Une valse a mis l' temps
De patienter vingt ans,
Pour que tu aies vingt ans
Et pour que j'aie vingt ans
Une valse à mille temps
Une valse à mille temps
Une valse à mille temps
Offre seule aux amants
Trois cent trente-trois fois le temps
De bâtir un roman

Au troisième temps de la valse
Nous valsons enfin tous les trois

Au troisième temps de la valse
Il y a toi y'a l'amour et y'a moi
Et Paris qui bat la mesure
Paris qui mesure notre émoi
Et Paris qui bat la mesure
Laisse enfin éclater sa joie

Une valse à trois temps
Qui s'offre encore le temps
Qui s'offre encore le temps
De s'offrir des détours
Du côté de l'amour
Comme c'est charmant
Une valse à quatre temps
C'est beaucoup moins dansant
C'est beaucoup moins dansant
Mais tout aussi charmant
Qu'une valse à trois temps
Une valse à quatre temps
Une valse à vingt temps
C'est beaucoup plus troublant
C'est beaucoup plus troublant
C'est beaucoup plus charmant
Qu'une valse à trois temps
Une valse à vingt ans
Une valse à cent temps
Une valse à cent temps
Une valse ça s'entend
A chaque carrefour
Dans Paris que l'amour
Rafraîchit au printemps
Une valse à mille temps
Une valse à mille temps
Une valse a mis l' temps
De patienter vingt ans
Pour que tu aies vingt ans
Et pour que j'aie vingt ans
Une valse à mille temps
Une valse à mille temps

Une valse à mille temps
Offre seule aux amants
Trois cent trente-trois fois le temps
De bâtir un roman.

IF WE ONLY HAVE LOVE [49]

If we only have love
Then tomorrow will dawn
And the days of our years
Will rise on that morn

If we only have love
To embrace without fears
We will kiss with our eyes
We will sleep without tears

If we only have love
With our arms open wide
Then the young and the old
Will stand at our side

If we only have love
Love that's falling like rain
Then the parched desert earth
Will grow green again

If we only have love
For the hymn that we shout

For the song that we sing
Then we'll have a way out

If we only have love
We can reach those in pain
We can heal all our wounds
We can use our own names

If we only have love
We can melt all the guns
And then give the new world
To our daughters and sons

If we only have love
Then Jerusalem stands
And then death has no shadow
There are no foreign lands

If we only have love
We will never bow down
We'll be tall as the pines
Neither heroes nor clowns

If we only have love
Then we'll only be men
And we'll drink from the Grail
To be born once again

Then with nothing at all
But the little we are
We'll have conquered all time
All space, the sun, and the stars.

QUAND ON N'A QUE L'AMOUR [50]

Quand on n'a que l'amour
A s'offrir en partage
Au jour du grand voyage
Qu'est notre grand amour
Quand on n'a que l'amour
Mon amour toi et moi
Pour qu'éclatent de joie
Chaque heure et chaque jour
Quand on n'a que l'amour
Pour vivre nos promesses
Sans nulle autre richesse
Que d'y croire toujours
Quand on n'a que l'amour
Pour meubler de merveilles
Et couvrir de soleil
La laideur des faubourgs
Quand on n'a que l'amour
Pour unique raison
Pour unique chanson
Et unique secours

Quand on n'a que l'amour
Pour habiller matin
Pauvres et malandrins
De manteaux de velours
Quand on n'a que l'amour
A offrir en prière
Pour les maux de la terre
En simple troubadour

Quand on n'a que l'amour
A offrir à ceux-là
Dont l'unique combat
Est de chercher le jour

Quand on n'a que l'amour
Pour tracer un chemin
Et forcer le destin
A chaque carrefour
Quand on n'a que l'amour
Pour parler aux canons
Et rien qu'une chanson
Pour convaincre un tambour

Alors sans avoir rien
Que la force d'aimer
Nous aurons dans nos mains,
Amis le monde entier